WITHDRAWN

BUOYANT BILLIONS

FARFETCHED FABLES

SHAKES VERSUS SHAV

➤➤➤⧫⧫⧫

BERNARD SHAW

Buoyant Billions,
Farfetched Fables,
&
Shakes Versus Shav

Dodd, Mead & Company

NEW YORK

CONTENTS

V

CONTENTS

BUOYANT BILLIONS

A COMEDY OF NO MANNERS

LI

1947

PREFACE

I COMMIT this to print within a few weeks of completing my 92nd year. At such an age I should apologize for perpetrating another play or presuming to pontificate in any fashion. I can hardly walk through my garden without a tumble or two; and it seems out of all reason to believe that a man who cannot do a simple thing like that can practise the craft of Shakespear. Is it not a serious sign of dotage to talk about oneself, which is precisely what I am now doing? Should it not warn me that my bolt is shot, and my place silent in the chimney corner?

Well, I grant all this; yet I cannot hold my tongue nor my pen. As long as I live I must write. If I stopped writing I should die for want of something to do.

If I am asked why I have written this play I must reply that I do not know. Among the many sects of Peculiar People which England produces so eccentrically and capriciously are the Spiritualists. They believe in personal immortality as far as any mortal can believe in an unimaginable horror. They have a cohort of Slate Writers and Writing Mediums in whose hands a pencil of any sort will, apparently of its own volition, write communications, undreamt-of by the medium, that must, they claim, be supernatural. It is objected to these that they have neither novelty, profundity, literary value nor artistic charm, being well within the capacity of very ordinary mortals, and are therefore dismissed as fraudulent on the ground that it is much more probable that the mediums are pretending and lying than performing miracles.

As trueblue Britons the mediums do not know how to defend themselves. They only argue-bargue. They should simply point out that the same objection may be raised against any famous scripture. For instance, the Peculiars known as Baconians believe, with all the evidence against them, that the plays attributed to Shakespear must have been written by somebody else, being unaccountably beyond his knowledge and capacity. Who that somebody else was is the mystery; for the plays are equally beyond the capacity of Bacon and all the later rival claimants. Our

3

greatest masterpiece of literature is the Jacobean translation of the Bible; and this the Christian Churches declare to be the word of God, supernaturally dictated through Christian mediums and transcribed by them as literally as any letter dictated by a merchant to his typist.

Take my own case. There is nothing in my circumstances or personality to suggest that I differ from any other son of a downstart gentleman driven by lack of unearned income to become an incompetent merchant and harp on his gentility. When I take my pen or sit down to my typewriter, I am as much a medium as Browning's Mr Sludge or Dunglas Home, or as Job or John of Patmos. When I write a play I do not foresee nor intend a page of it from one end to the other: the play writes itself. I may reason out every sentence until I have made it say exactly what it comes to me to say; but whence and how and why it comes to me, or why I persisted, through nine years of unrelieved market failure, in writing instead of in stockbroking or turf bookmaking or peddling, I do not know. You may say it was because I had a talent that way. So I had; but that fact remains inexplicable. What less could Mr Sludge say? or John Hus, who let himself be burnt rather than recant his "I dont know. Instruct me"?

When I was a small boy I saw a professional writing medium, pencil in hand, slash down page after page with astonishing speed without lifting his pencil from the blank paper we fed on to his desk. The fact that he was later transported for forgery did not make his performance and his choice of mediumship as his profession less unaccountable. When I was an elderly man, my mother amused herself with a planchette and a ouija, which under her hands produced what are called spirit writings abundantly. It is true that these screeds might have been called wishful writings (like wishful thinkings) so clearly were they as much her own story-telling inventions as the Waverley novels were Scott's. But why did she choose and practise this senseless activity? Why was I doing essentially the same as a playwright? I do not know. We both got some satisfaction from it or we would not have done it.

This satisfaction, this pleasure, this appetite, is as yet far from being as intense as the sexual orgasm or the ecstasy of a saint, though future cortical evolution may leave them far behind. Yet there are the moments of inexplicable happiness of which Mr J. B. Priestley spoke in a recent broadcast as part of his experience. To me they have come only in dreams not oftener than once every fifteen years or so. I do not know how common they are; for I never heard anyone but Mr Priestley mention them. They have an exalted chronic happiness, as of earth become heaven, proving that such states are possible for us even as we now are.

The happiest moment of my life was when as a child I was told by my mother that we were going to move from our Dublin street to Dalkey Hill in sight of the skies and seas of the two great bays between Howth and Bray, with Dalkey Island in the middle. I had already had a glimpse of them, and of Glencree in the mountains, on Sunday excursions; and they had given me the magic delight Mr Ivor Brown has described as the effect on him of natural scenery. Let who can explain it. Poets only can express it. It is a hard fact, waiting for some scientific genius to make psychology of it.

The professional biologists tell us nothing of all this. It would take them out of the realm of logic into that of magic and miracle, in which they would lose their reputation for omniscience and infallibility. But magic and miracle, as far as they are not flat lies, are not divorced from facts and consequently from science: they are facts: as yet unaccounted for, but none the less facts. As such they raise problems; and genuine scientists must face them at the risk of being classed with Cagliostro instead of with Clerk-Maxwell and Einstein, Galileo and Newton, who, by the way, worked hard at interpreting the Bible, and was ashamed of his invention of the Infinitesimal Calculus until Leibniz made it fashionable.

Now Newton was right in rating the Calculus no higher than a schoolboy's crib, and the interpretation of The Bible as far more important. In this valuation, which seems so queer to us today, he was not in the least lapsing from science into superstition: he was looking for the foundation of literary art in the facts of history. Nothing could be more important or more scientific; and the fact that the result was the most absurd book in the English language (his Chronology) does not invalidate in the least his integrity as a scientific investigator, nor exemplify his extraordinary mental gifts any less than his hypothesis of gravitation, which might have occurred to anyone who had seen an apple fall when he was wondering why moving bodies did not move in straight lines away into space. Newton was no farther off the scientific target in his attribution of infallibility to Archbishop Ussher than most modern biologists and self-styled scientific socialists in their idolatry of Darwin and Marx. The scientist who solves the problem of the prophet Daniel and John of Patmos, and incidentally of Shakespear and myself, will make a longer stride ahead than any solver of physical problems.

My readers keep complaining in private letters and public criticisms that I have not solved all the problems of the universe for them. As I am obviously neither omnipotent, omniscient, nor infallible, being not only not a god nor even the proprietor of The Times (as they all assume), they infuriate me. Instead of reminding them calmly that, like Newton, all I know is but a grain of sand picked up on the verge of the ocean of undiscovered knowledge, I have some difficulty in refraining from some paraphrase of "An evil and idolatrous generation clamors for a miracle." But as Mahomet kept his temper under the same thoughtless pressure, so, I suppose, must I.

This is all I can write by way of preface to a trivial comedy which is the best I can do in my dotage. It is only a prefacette to a comedietta. Forgive it. At least it will not rub into you the miseries and sins of the recent wars, nor even of the next one. History will make little of them; and the sooner we forget them the better. I wonder how many people really prefer bogus war news and police news to smiling comedy with some hope in it! I do not. When they begin I switch off the wireless.

Ayot Saint Lawrence,
July 1947

6

ACT I

THE WORLD BETTERER

A *MODERN interior. A well furnished study. Morn-*
ing light. A father discussing with his son. Father
an elderly gentleman, evidently prosperous, but a
man of business, thoroughly middle class. Son in his earliest
twenties, smart, but artistically unconventional.

FATHER. Junius, my boy, you must make up your mind.
I had a long talk with your mother about it last night. You
have been tied to her apron string quite long enough. You
have been on my hands much too long. Your six brothers
all chose their professions when they were years younger
than you. I have always expected more from you than from
them. So has your mother.

SON. Why?

FATHER. I suppose because you are our seventh son;
and I myself was a seventh son. You are the seventh son of
a seventh son. You ought to have second sight.

SON. I have. At first sight there is no hope for our civilization. But one can still make money in it. At second sight
the world has a future that will make its people look back on
us as a mob of starving savages. But second sight does not
yet lead to success in business nor in the professions.

FATHER. That is not so. You have done unusually well
at everything you have tried. You were a success at school.
I was assured that you had the makings of a born leader
of men in you.

SON. Yes. They made me a prefect and gave me a cane
to beat the boys they were too lazy to beat themselves. That
was what they called teaching me leadership.

FATHER. Well, it gave you some sense of responsibility:
what more could they do? At the university you did not do
so well; but you could have if you had chosen to work for
honors instead of joining rather disreputable clubs and
working on your own lines, as you called them. As it was,
you did not disgrace yourself. We looked to you to outshine

7

your brothers. But they are all doing well; and you are doing nothing.

SON. I know. But the only profession that appeals to me is one that I cannot afford.

FATHER. How do you know that you cannot afford it? Have I ever stinted you in any way? Do you suppose I expect you to establish yourself in a profession or business in five minutes?

SON. No: you have always been a model father. But the profession I contemplate is not one that a model father could recommend to his son.

FATHER. And what profession is that, pray?

SON. One that is always unsuccessful. Marx's profession. Lenin's profession. Stalin's profession. Ruskin's profession. Plato's profession. Confucius, Gautama, Jesus, Mahomet, Luther, William Morris. The profession of world betterer.

FATHER. My boy, great prophets and poets are all very well; but they are not practical men; and what we need are practical men.

SON. We dont get them. We need men who can harness the tides and the tempests, atom splitting engineers, mathematicians, biologists, psychologists. What do we get? Windbag careerists. Proletarians who can value money in shillings but not in millions, and think their trade unions are the world. As a world betterer I shall spend most of my life hiding from their police. And I may finish on the scaffold.

FATHER. Romantic nonsense, boy. You are in a free country, and can advocate any sort of politics you please as long as you do not break the law.

SON. But I want to break the law.

FATHER. You mean change the law. Well, you can advocate any change you please; and if you can persuade us all to agree with you, you can get elected to Parliament and bring your changes before the House of Commons.

SON. Too slow. Class war is rushing on us with tiger springs. The tiger has sprung in Russia, in Persia, in Mexico, in Turkey, in Italy, Spain, Germany, Austria, everywhere if you count national strikes as acts of civil war. We are trying to charm the tiger away by mumbling old spells about liberty, peace, democracy, sanctions, open doors, and closed minds, when it is scientific political reconstruction that is called for. So I propose to become a political reconstructionist. Are you in favor of reconstruction?

FATHER. I do not see any need for it. All the people who are discontented are so because they are poor. I am not poor; and I do not see why I should be discontented.

SON. Well, I am discontented because other people are poor. To me living in a world of poor and unhappy people is like living in hell.

FATHER. You need not speak to them. You need not know them. You do not mix with them. And they are not unhappy.

SON. How am I to get away from them? The streets are full of them. And how do I know that we shall not lose all our money and fall into poverty ourselves? Fancy you and mother ending your days in a workhouse, or trying to live on an old age pension! That happens, you know.

FATHER. In our case it happens the other way. There is no need to mention it outside; but one of my grandfathers, the founder of our present fortune, began as a porter in a hotel. Thanks to his ability and the social system that gave it scope, we are now safely fixed in a social circle where rich men become richer instead of poorer if they are sensible and well conducted. Our system works very satisfactorily. Why reconstruct it?

SON. Many people feel like that. Others feel as I do. If neither of us will budge, and no compromise is possible, what are we to do? Kill oneanother?

FATHER. Nonsense! There are constitutional ways of making all possible political changes.

SON. Voting instead of fighting. No use. The defeated party always fights if it has a dog's chance when the point is worth fighting for and it can find a leader. The defeated dictator always fights unless his successor takes the precaution of murdering him.

FATHER. Not in England. Such things happen only on the Continent. We don't do them here.

SON. We do. We did it in Ireland. We did it in India. It has always been so. We resist changes until the changes break us.

FATHER. Well, what does all this come to? If people wont change what good is there in your being a world betterer, as you call it?

SON. What good is there in going on as we are? Besides, things will not stay as they are. However hard we try to stick in our old grooves, evolution goes on in spite of us. The more we strive to stay as we are, the more we find that we are no longer where we were.

FATHER. Yet we are not always having revolutions.

SON. They occur, though nobody understands them. When the feudal aristocracy collapsed before the plutocratic middle class Henry the Seventh had to fight the battle of Bosworth Field. When the plutocrats got the upper hand of the monarchy Cromwell had to cut off the king's head. The French Revolution tried hard to be Liberal and Parliamentary. No use: the guillotine was overworked until the executioners struck; and Napoleon had to fight all Europe. When the Russians did away with the Tzardom they had to fight not only all the rest of the world but a civil war as well. They first killed all the counter-revolutionists; and then had to kill most of the revolutionists. Revolution is dirty work always. Why should it be?

FATHER. Because it is unconstitutional. Why not do things constitutionally?

SON. Because the object of a revolution is to change the constitution; and to change the constitution is unconstitutional.

FATHER. That is a quibble. It is always possible to vote instead of fighting. All the blood shed in revolutions has been quite unnecessary. All the changes could have been effected without killing anybody. You must listen to reason?

SON. Yes; but reason leads just as clearly to a catholic monarchy as to an American republic, to a Communist Soviet as to Capitalism. What is the use of arguing when the Pope's arguments are as logical as Martin Luther's, and Hilaire Belloc's as H. G. Wells's? Why appeal to the mob when ninetyfive per cent of them do not understand politics, and can do nothing but mischief without leaders? And what sort of leaders do they vote for? For Titus Oates and Lord George Gordon with their Popish plots, for Hitlers who call on them to exterminate Jews, for Mussolinis who rally them to nationalist dreams of glory and empire in which all foreigners are enemies to be subjugated.

FATHER. The people run after wicked leaders only when they cannot find righteous ones. They can always find them in England.

SON. Yes; and when they find them why do they run after them? Only to crucify them. The righteous man takes his life in his hand whenever he utters the truth. Charlemagne, Mahomet, St Dominic: these were righteous men according to their lights; but with Charlemagne it was embrace Christianity instantly or die; with Mahomet the slaying of the infidel was a passport to Heaven; with Dominic and his Dogs of God it was Recant or burn.

FATHER. But these things happened long ago, when people were cruel and uncivilized.

SON. My dear father: within the last thirty years we have had more horrible persecutions and massacres, more diabolical tortures and crucifixions, more slaughter and destruction than Attila and Genghis Khan and all the other scourges of God ever ventured on. I tell you, if people only knew the history of their own times they would die of horror at their own wickedness. Karl Marx changed the mind of the world by simply telling the purseproud nineteenth century its own villainous history. He ruined himself; his infant son died of poverty; and two of his children committed suicide. But he did the trick.

FATHER. The Russian madness will not last. Indeed it has collapsed already. I now invest all my savings in Russian Government Stock. My stockbroker refuses to buy it for me; but my banker assures me that it is the only perfectly safe foreign investment. The Russians pay in their own gold.

SON. And the gold goes to rot in American banks, though whole nations are barely keeping half alive for lack of it.

FATHER. Well, my boy, you are keeping alive pretty comfortably. Why should you saw through the branch you are sitting on?

SON. Because it is cracking; and it seems to me prudent to arrange a soft place to drop to when it snaps.

FATHER. The softest place now is where you are. Listen to me, my boy. You are cleverer than I am. You know more. You know too much. You talk too well. I have thought a good deal over this. I have tried to imagine what old John Shakespear of Stratford-upon-Avon, mayor and alderman and leading citizen of his town, must have felt when he declined into bankruptcy and realized that his good-for-nothing son, who had run away to London after his conviction as a poacher, and being forced to marry a girl he had compromised, was a much greater man than his father had ever been or could hope to be. That is what may happen to me. But there is a difference. Shakespear had a lucrative talent by which he prospered and returned to his native town as a rich man, and bought a property there. You have no such talent. I cannot start you in life with a gift of capital as I started your brothers, because the war taxation has left me barely enough to pay my own way. I can do nothing for you: if you want to better the world you must begin by bettering yourself.

SON. And until I better the world I cannot better myself; for nobody will employ a world betterer as long as there are enough selfseekers for all the paying jobs. Still, some of the world betterers manage to survive. Why not I?

FATHER. They survive because they fit themselves into the world of today. They marry rich women. They take commercial jobs. They spunge on disciples from whom they beg or borrow. What else can they do except starve or commit suicide? A hundred years ago there were kings to spunge on. Nowadays there are republics everywhere; and their governments are irresistible, because they alone can afford to make atomic bombs, and wipe out a city and all its inhabitants in a thousandth of a second.

SON. What does that matter if they can build it again in

ten minutes? All the scientists in the world are at work finding out how to dilute and control and cheapen atomic power until it can be used to boil an egg or sharpen a lead pencil as easily as to destroy a city. Already they tell us that the bomb stuff will make itself for nothing.

FATHER. I hope not. For if every man Jack of us can blow the world to pieces there will be an end of everything. Shakespear's angry ape will see to that.

SON. Will he? He hasnt done so yet. I can go into the nearest oil shop and for less than a shilling buy enough chemical salts to blow this house and all its inhabitants to smithereens. A glass retort, a pestle and mortar, and a wash bottle are all I need to do the trick. But I dont do it.

FATHER. The trade unions did it in Manchester and Sheffield.

SON. They soon dropped it. They did not even destroy the slums they lived in: they only blew up a few of their own people for not joining the unions. No: mankind has not the nerve to go through to the end with murder and suicide. Hiroshima and Nagasaki are already rebuilt; and Japan is all the better for the change. When atom splitting makes it easy for us to support ourselves as well by two hours work as now by two years, we shall move mountains and straighten rivers in a hand's turn. Then the problem of what to do in our spare time will make life enormously more interesting. No more doubt as to whether life is worth living. Then the world betterers will come to their own.

FATHER. The sportsmen will, anyhow. War is a sport. It used to be the sport of kings. Now it is the sport of Labor Parties.

SON. What could kings and parties do without armies of proletarians? War is a sport too ruinous and vicious for men ennobled by immense power and its splendid possibilities.

FATHER. Power corrupts: it does not ennoble.

SON. It does if it is big enough. It is petty power that corrupts petty men. Almighty power will change the world. If the old civilizations, the Sumerians, the Egyptians, the Greeks, the Romans, had discovered it, their civilizations would not have collapsed as they did. There would have been no Dark Ages. The world betterers will get the upper hand.

FATHER. Well, it may be so. But does not that point to your settling down respectably as an atom splitting engineer with the government and the police on your side?

SON. Yes, if only I had any talent for it. But I seem to have no talent for anything but preaching and propaganda. I am a missionary without an endowed established Church.

FATHER. Then how are you to live? You must do something to support yourself when I am gone.

SON. I have thought of insuring your life.

FATHER. How are you to pay the premium?

SON. Borrow it from mother, I suppose.

FATHER. Well, there is some sense in that. But it would not last your lifetime: it would only give you a start. At what?

SON. I could speak in the parks until I attracted a congregation of my own. Then I could start a proprietary chapel and live on the collections.

FATHER. And this is what I am to tell your mother!

SON. If I were you I wouldnt.

FATHER. Oh, you are incorrigible. I tell you again you are too clever: you know too much: I can do nothing with you. I wonder how many fathers are saying the same to their sons today.

SON. Lots of them. In your time the young were post-Marxists and their fathers pre-Marxists. Today we are all post-Atomists.

FATHER. Damn the atomic bomb!

SON. Bless it say I. It will make world bettering possible. It will begin by ridding the world of the anopheles mosquito, the tsetse fly, the white ant, and the locust. I want to go round the world to investigate that, especially through the Panama Canal. Will you pay my fare?

FATHER. Yes: anything to keep you from tomfooling in the parks. And it will keep your mother quiet for a while.

SON. Better say nothing until I am gone. She would

never let me go: her seventh son is her pet. It is a tyranny from which I must escape.

FATHER. And leave me to weather the storm! Well, goodbye.

SON. Goodbye. You are a damned good father; and I shall not forget it.

They kiss; and the son goes.

ACT II
THE ADVENTURE

THE shore of a broad water studded with half-submerged trees in a tropical landscape, covered with bush except for a clearance by the waterside, where there is a wooden house on posts, with a ladder from the stoep or verandah to the ground. The roof is of corrugated iron, painted green. The Son, dressed in flannel slacks, a tennis shirt, and a panama hat, is looking about him like a stranger. A young woman, dressed for work in pyjama slacks and a pullover, comes out of the house and, from the top of the steps, proceeds to make the stranger unwelcome.

SHE. Now then. This clearance is private property. Whats your business?

HE. No business, dear lady. Treat me as a passing tramp.

SHE. Well, pass double quick. This isnt a doss house.

HE. No; but in this lonely place the arrival of any stranger must be a godsend. Besides, I am hungry and thirsty.

SHE. Most tramps are. Get out.

HE. No: positively no, until I have had refreshments.

SHE. I have a dog here.

HE. You have not. It would have barked. And dogs love me.

SHE. I have a gun here.

HE. So have I. Both useless, except to commit suicide. Have you a husband?

SHE. What is that to you?

HE. If you have, he is only a man, lady. I also am a man. But you do not look married. Have you any milk in the house? Or a hunk of bread and an onion?

SHE. Not for you.

HE. Why not? Have you any religion?

SHE. No. Get out.

HE. Ah, that complicates matters. I thought you were a hospitable friendly savage. I see you are a commercial minded British snob. Must I insult you by offering to pay for my entertainment? Or impress you by introducing myself as a graduate of Oxford University?

16

SHE. I know that stunt, my lad. The wandering scholar turns up here about twice a week.

HE. "My lad" eh? That is an endearment. We are getting on. What about the milk?

SHE. You can get a meal where the lake steamers stop, two miles farther on.

HE. Two miles! In this heat! I should die.

SHE [*patiently*] Will you pass on and not come troubling where you are not wanted. [*She goes into the house and slams the door*].

An elderly native arrives with a jar of milk and a basket of bread and fruit. He deposits them on the stoep.

THE NATIVE [*calling to the lady inside*] Ahaiya! Missy's rations. Pink person loafing round.

She opens the door and hands a coin to the native; then slams the door before, after an angry glance at the intruder, leaving the meal on the stoep.

HE [*to the native*] You bring me samee. Half dollar. [*He exhibits the coin*].

THE NATIVE. Too much. Twentyfive cent enough.

HE [*producing a 25c. piece and giving it to him*] The honest man gets paid in advance and has his part in the glory of God.

THE NATIVE. You wait here. No walk about.

HE. Why not?

THE NATIVE. Not good walk about. Gater and snake.

HE. What is gater?

THE NATIVE. Alligator, sir. Much gater, much rattler.

HE. All right. I wait here.

THE NATIVE. Yes, sir. And you no speak holy woman. Speak to her forbidden. She speak with great spirits only. Very strong magics. Put spell on you. Fetch gaters and rattlers with magic tunes on her pipe. Very unlucky speak to her. Very lucky bring her gifts.

HE. Has she husband?

THE NATIVE. No no no no. She holy woman. Live alone. You no speak to her, sir. You wait here. Back quick with chop chop. [*He goes*].

SHE [*opening the door again*] Not gone yet?

HE. The native says you are a holy woman. You are treating me in a very unholy manner. May I suggest that you allow me to consume your meal? You can consume mine yourself after he brings it? I am hungrier than you.

SHE. You are not starving. A fast will do you no harm. You can wait ten minutes more at all events. If you persist in bothering me I will call the gaters and the rattlers.

HE. You have been listening. That is another advance.

SHE. Take care. I can call them.

HE. How?

SHE. In the days of my vanity, when I tried to be happy with men like you, I learnt how to play the soprano saxophone. I have the instrument here. Twenty notes from it will surround you with hissing rattling things, with gaping jaws and slashing tails. I am far better protected against idle gentlemen here than I should be in Piccadilly.

HE. Yes, holy lady; but what about your conscience? A hungry man asks you for food. Dare you throw him to the gaters and rattlers? How will that appear in the great day of reckoning?

SHE. Neither you nor I will matter much when that day comes, if it ever does. But you can eat my lunch to shut your mouth.

HE. Oh, thanks!

SHE. You need not look round for a tumbler and a knife and fork. Drink from the calabash: eat from your fingers.

HE. The simple life, eh? [*He attacks the meal.*]

SHE. No. In the simple life you ring for the servants. Everything is done for you; and you learn nothing.

HE. And here you wait until that kindly native comes and feeds you, like Elijah's ravens. What do you learn from that?

SHE. You learn what nice people natives are. But you begin by trying to feed yourself and build your own shack. I have been through all that, and learnt what a helpless creature a civilized woman is.

HE. Quite. That is the advantage of being civilized: everything is done for you by somebody else; and you havnt a notion of how or why, unless you read Karl Marx.

SHE. I read Karl Marx when I was fifteen. That is why I am here instead of in London looking for a rich husband.

HE. We are getting on like old friends. Evidently I please you.

SHE. Why do you want to please me now that you have your meal?

HE. I dont know. Why do we go on talking to one-another?

SHE. I dont know. We are dangerous to oneanother. Finish your food; and pass on.

HE. But you have chosen to live dangerously. So have I. It may break our hearts if I pass on.

SHE. Young man: I spent years waiting for somebody to break my heart before I discovered that I havnt got one. I broke several men's hearts in the process. I came here to get rid of that sort of thing. I can stand almost anything human except an English gentleman.

HE. And I can stand anything except an English lady. That game is up. Dancing and gambling, drinking cocktails, tempting women and running away when they meet you half-way and say "Thats quite all right, sonny: dont apologize." Hunting and shooting is all right; but you need to be a genuine countrified savage for it; and I am a town bird. My father is a chain shopkeeper, not a country squire.

SHE. Same here: my father is a famous lucky financier. Born a proletarian. Neither of us the real thing.

HE. Plenty of money and no roots. No traditions.

SHE. Nonsense. We are rooted in the slums and suburbs, and full of their snobbery. But failures as ladies and gentlemen.

HE. Nothing left but to live on father's money, eh?

SHE. Yes: parasites: that is not living. Yet we have our living selves for all that. And in this wild life you can taste yourself.

HE. Not always a pleasant taste, is it?

SHE. Every animal can bear its own odor.

HE. That remark has completely destroyed my appetite. The coarse realism with which women face physical facts shocks the delicacy of my sex.

SHE. Yes: men are dreamers and drones. So if you can eat no more, get out.

HE. I should much prefer to lie down and sleep in the friendly shadow of your house until the heat of the day has done its worst.

SHE. If you want a house to shade you, build one for yourself. Leave mine in peace.

HE. That is not natural. In native life the woman keeps the house and works there: the man keeps the woman and rests there.

SHE. You do not keep the woman in this case. She has had enough of you. Get out.

HE. As I see things the woman does not say get out.

SHE. Do you expect her to say come in? As you see things, the man works out of doors. What does he work at, pray?

HE. He hunts, fishes, and fights.

SHE. Have you hunted or fished for me?

HE. No. I hate killing.

SHE. Have you fought for me?

HE. No. I am a timid creature.

SHE. Cowards are no use to women. They need killers. Where are your scalps?

HE. My what?

SHE. Your trophies that you dare kill. The scalps of our enemies.

HE. I have never killed anybody. I dont want to. I want a decent life for everybody because poor people are as tiresome as rich people.

SHE. What is the woman to eat if you do not kill animals for her?

HE. She can be a vegetarian. I am.

SHE. So am I. But I have learnt here that if we vegetarians do not kill animals the animals will kill us. It is the flesh eaters who let the animals live, and feed and nurse them. We vegetarians will make an end of them. No matter what we eat, man is still the killer and woman the life giver. Can you kill or not?

20

HE. I can shoot a little, though few experienced country gentlemen would care to be next to me at a shoot. But I do not know how to load the gun: I must have a loader. I cannot find the birds: they have to be driven to me by an army of beaters. And I expect a good lunch afterwards. I can also hunt if somebody will fetch me a saddled horse, and stable it for me and take it off my hands again when the hunt is over. I should be afraid not to fight if you put me into an army and convinced me that if I ran away I should be shot at dawn. But of what use are these heroic accomplishments here? No loaders, no beaters, no grooms, no stables, no soldiers, no King and country. I should have to learn to make bows and arrows and assegais; to track game; to catch and break-in wild horses; and to tackle natives armed with poisoned arrows. I should not have a dog's chance. There are only two things I can do as well as any native: eat and sleep. You have enabled me to eat. Why will you not let me sleep?

SHE. Because I want to practise on the saxophone. The rattlers will come and you will never awake.

HE. Then hadnt you better let me sleep indoors?

SHE. The saxophone would keep you awake.

HE. On the contrary, music always sends me fast asleep.

SHE. The only sleep that is possible here when I am playing the saxophone is the sleep of death.

HE [*rising wearily*] You have the last word. You are an inhospitable wretch.

SHE. And you are an infernal nuisance [*she goes into the house and slams the door*].

The native returns with another meal. He puts it down near the door, at which he raps.

THE NATIVE [*cries*] Ahaiya! Missy's meal.

HE. Say, John: can you direct me to the nearest witch doctor? Spell maker. One who can put terrible strong magics on this house.

THE NATIVE. Sir: magics are superstitions. Pink trash believe such things: colored man, no.

HE. But havnt you gods and priests who can bring down the anger of the gods on unkind people?

THE NATIVE. Sir: there is but one god, the source of all creation. His dwelling is in the sun: therefore though you can look upon all other things you cannot look at the sun.

HE. What do you call him?

THE NATIVE. Sir: his name is not to be pronounced without great reverence. I have been taught that he has other names in other lands; but here his holy name [*he bends his neck*] is Hoochlipoochli. He has a hundred earthly brides; and she who dwells within is one of them.

HE. Listen to me, John. We white men have a god much much greater than Hoochlipoochli.

THE NATIVE. Sir: that may be so. But you pink men do not believe in your god. We believe in ours. Better have no god at all than a god in whom you do not believe.

HE. What do you mean by our not believing? How do you know we do not believe?

THE NATIVE. He who believes in his god, obeys his commands. You expect your god to obey yours. But pardon me, sir: I am forbidden to converse on such high matters with the unlearned. I perceive by your assurance that you are a highly honorable person among your own people; but here you are a heathen, a barbarian, an infidel. Mentally we are not on the same plane. Conversation between us, except on such simple matters as milk and vegetables, could lead only to bewilderment and strife. I wish you good morning, sir.

HE. Stay, presumptuous one. I would have you to know that I am a Master of Arts of the University of Oxford, the centre of all the learning in the universe. The possession of such a degree places the graduate on the highest mental plane attainable by humanity.

THE NATIVE. How did you obtain that degree, sir, may I respectfully ask?

HE. By paying a solid twenty pounds for it.

THE NATIVE. It is impossible. Knowledge and wisdom cannot be purchased like fashionable garments.

HE. In England they can. A sage teaches us all the questions our examiners are likely to ask us, and the answers they expect from us.

THE NATIVE. One answers questions truthfully only out of one's own wisdom and knowledge.

HE. Not at Oxford. Unless you are a hundred years behindhand in science and seven hundred in history you cannot hope for a degree there.

THE NATIVE. Can it be true that the doctrines of your teachers are less than a thousand years old?

HE. The most advanced of them would have felt quite at home with Richard the Third. I should like to have heard them discussing Columbus with him.

THE NATIVE. Then, sir, you must indeed venerate me; for the doctrines of my teachers have lasted many thousands of centuries. Only the truth could survive so long.

HE. I venerate nobody. Veneration is dead. Oxford doctrine has made a gentleman of me. You, it seems, have been made a sage by a similar process. Are we any the better or wiser?

THE NATIVE. Sir: you have lost your faith; but do not throw the hatchet after the handle. Pink men, when they find that their beliefs are only half true, reject both halves. We colored men are more considerate. My grandfather saw the great evils of this world, and thought they shewed the terrible greatness of Hoochlipoochli. My father saw them also, but could not reconcile the existence of evil with divine justice and benevolence. He therefore believed not only in Hoochlipoochli but in Poochlihoochli, the god of hell, whom you pink men call The Devil. As for me, I cannot believe everything my ancestors believed. I believe as they did that justice and benevolence are mighty powers in the world, but that they have no effective existence save in ourselves, and that except to the extent to which you and I and our like are just and benevolent there is no justice and no benevolence.

HE. And consequently no Hoochlipoochli.

THE NATIVE. Not at all. You are throwing the hatchet after the handle. His kingdom is within us; but it is for us to administer it. Something within me makes me hunger and thirst for righteousness. That something must be Hoochlipoochli.

23

HE. Was it Hoochlipoochli who set you talking pidgin English to me though you can talk philosopher's English better than most Englishmen?

THE NATIVE. Sir: you began by speaking pidgin to me. You addressed me as John, which is not my name. In courtesy I spoke as you spoke.

HE. Still, when you told me that the woman here is one of Hoochlipoochli's many hundred earthly wives, you were humbugging me.

THE NATIVE. Sir: Hoochlipoochli possesses all of us more or less; and so every woman is his bride. I desired only your good when I bade you beware of her; for it is true that when she plays on her strange instrument the serpents of the bush and the monsters of the lake are charmed, and assemble here to listen.

SHE [*throwing open her door and appearing on the threshold with the saxophone in her hand*] And if you do not stop talking and maddening me with the sound of your cackle I shall strike up.

HE. Strike up by all means. I shall enjoy a little music.

SHE. We shall see. I have had enough of you.

She preludes on the saxophone.

Hissings and rattlings in the bush. An alligator crawls in. The two men fly for their lives.

ACT III
THE DISCUSSION

A DRAWINGROOM *in Belgrave Square, London, converted into a Chinese temple on a domestic scale, with white walls just enough rose tinted to take the glare off, and a tabernacle in vermilion and gold, on a dais of two broad shallow steps. Divan seats, softly upholstered against the walls, and very comfortable easy chairs of wickerwork, luxuriously cushioned, are also available. There is a sort of bishop's chair at one corner of the tabernacle. The effect is lovely and soothing, as only Chinese art could make it.*

A most incongruous figure enters: a middle-aged twentieth century London solicitor, carrying a case of papers. He is accompanied and ushered by a robed Chinese priest, who fits perfectly into the surroundings.

THE SOLICITOR [*looking round him*] Whats all this? I should have been shewn into the library. Do you understand who I am? Sir Ferdinand Flopper, Mr Buoyant's solicitor?

THE PRIEST. It is Mr Buoyant's wish that you should meet his children in this holy place. Did he not mention it in your instructions?

SIR FERDINAND. No. This place is not holy. We are in Belgrave Square, not in Hong Kong.

THE PRIEST. Sir: in many old English houses there is a room set apart as a meditation parlor.

SIR FERDINAND. Pooh! They have been abolished.

THE PRIEST. Yes. The English people no longer meditate.

SIR FERDINAND. Does Mr Buoyant?

THE PRIEST. His soul needs refreshment. He is a mighty man of business: in his hands all things turn into money. Souls perish under such burdens. He comes here and sits for half an hour while I go through my act of worship, of which he does not understand a single word. But he goes out a new man, soothed and serene. You may call this his oratory.

SIR FERDINAND. I shall certainly not call it anything of

25

the sort. His oratory would be a Church of England oratory.

THE PRIEST. He has not found peace in the Church of England.

SIR FERDINAND. And you tell me that he has found it here, in this outlandish apartment where he does not understand a word of the service!

THE PRIEST. In the Church of England he understood too much. He could not believe. And the people in their Sunday clothes were so forbidding!

SIR FERDINAND. Forbidding!!

THE PRIEST. Sunday clothes and poker faces. No peace, no joy. But for the music they would all go mad. That is, perhaps, why you do not go to church.

SIR FERDINAND. Who told you I do not go to church?

THE PRIEST. Nobody told me. But do you?

SIR FERDINAND. I am here on business, and cannot waste my morning on religious discussions. Will you be good enough to direct me to the library?

THE PRIEST. You would find it a rather dismal apartment after this one. And its atmosphere is mentally paralyzing. Mr Buoyant's instructions are that your advice to his family must be given here. But no religious service is to be imposed on you.

SIR FERDINAND. Nothing can be imposed on me. The atmosphere here is most unsuitable. Does the family know I have arrived?

THE PRIEST. Here they are.

The family, consisting of a middle-aged widower, a younger man, two married ladies, an unmarried girl of 20, and an irreverent youth of 17, enters. The widower introduces them.

THE WIDOWER. Good morning, Sir Ferdinand. We are the family of your client Mr Bastable Buoyant, better known as Old Bill Buoyant the Billionaire. I am a widower. The ladies are my brothers' wives. One brother is absent: he leaves everything to his wife. The two children are our sister Darkie and our brother Fiffy, registered as Eudoxia Emily and Frederick.

They bow to Sir Ferdinand as they are introduced, and

26

seat themselves on the divan, the husbands on opposite sides from their wives.

The two juniors also plant themselves on opposite sides well to the fore. Sir Ferdinand, returning their bows rather stiffly, seats himself in the bishop's chair.

THE PRIEST. I leave you to your deliberations. Peace be with you!

He goes, the family waving him a salute.

SIR FERDINAND. As I have only just been called in, and am a stranger to you all, I am naturally somewhat at a loss. How much do you know already of the business I am to put before you?

DARKIE [*taking the lead at once decisively*] Nothing whatever. Business means money; and none of us knows anything about money because our father knows everything about it. But I know all about housekeeping because our mother knew nothing about it and cared less. She preferred painting. We had extraordinarily clever parents; and the result is that we are a family of helpless duffers.

SECONDBORN. That is true. So much has been done for us we have learnt to do hardly anything for ourselves. I am a bit of a mathematician, but earn nothing by it.

MRS SECONDBORN [*an aggressive woman*] Mathematics; that is his fad. Start a Buoyant on a fad; and he is happy and busy with it for the rest of the year.

THE YOUTH. We are too damnably rich, you see. The boss making billions all the time.

DARKIE. We have bits and scraps of tastes and talents for scholarship, painting, playing musical instruments, writing, and talking. One brother is a champion amateur boxer. Another is a historian and knows eleven languages. He is also a pedestrian and walks 3000 miles every year on principle. We are all more or less like that, because daddy began with eight shillings a week and taught himself to read and write when he was seventeen and wanted to write to his mother. She could read handwriting.

THE WIDOWER. Darkie is explaining to you that as we are entirely dependent on our father for our incomes we can defend ourselves against his tyranny only by acquiring the

27

culture of which an uneducated man stands in awe.

MRS THIRDBORN [*gentle, beautiful, and saintly*] Oh, he is not a tyrant.

THE WIDOWER. He might be, if we were not obviously his social superiors.

MRS SECONDBORN. In justice to the old devil I must say that, as far as I can make out, he has never spoken a cross word to any of you.

DARKIE. I never said he did. I was going to explain my own exceptional position in the family. Am I boring you, Sir Ferdinand?

SIR FERDINAND. Not at all. We have plenty of time before lunch. So if your position is exceptional, I had better know what it is.

DARKIE. Well, as I am the only female, I am the spoilt darling and pampered pet of the lot. I have no talents, no accomplishments, except what I picked up doing just what I liked and was given everything I asked for. That has been harder than any schooling; and I sometimes blame my parents for not having thrashed the life out of me instead of leaving me to learn life's lessons by breaking my shins against them and falling into every booby trap. I was so overpetted that I had to learn or die. So if there is anything real to be done I have to see to it.

MRS THIRDBORN [*very kindly*] Dont mind her, Sir Ferdinand. She always talks the greatest nonsense about herself.

DARKIE. I daresay I do. Anyhow I have finished now. Go ahead, Sir Ferdinand.

SIR FERDINAND. One question first please. Mr Buoyant must have had legal advice during all these years. Is there not a family solicitor?

THE WIDOWER. No. He does not believe in having the same solicitor every time.

DARKIE. He thinks it is throwing away experience. He always calls in a different doctor when he is ill.

THE YOUTH. He picks up his solicitor for the job, like picking up a taxi.

THE WIDOWER. There is something to be said for his

plan. He has learnt much about doctors and solicitors by it.

SECONDBORN. He now advises his doctors and instructs his solicitors.

SIR F. If so, why does he call them in at all?

MRS SECONDBORN. If he didnt, and any of us died, or any money he is trustee for went wrong, he might be prosecuted for negligence or conversion or something.

SIR F. True. But this raises questions of professional etiquet. I have some misgivings as to whether I can act in the case.

THE YOUTH. If the boss says you can, you may bet your bottom dollar it will be all right.

DARKIE. He makes so much money that whatever he says, goes.

SIR F. Not legally.

THE WIDOWER. No doubt. But it works pragmatically.

SIR F. I hardly know what to say. You are such an unusually outspoken family, and your father such an extraordinary man, that I should like to know more of you. You belong to a new generation, quite unlike mine. I am at sea here. May I continue provisionally as a friendly acquaintance rather than as a solicitor?

DARKIE. The very thing!

THE YOUTH. Silence all.

DARKIE. Go ahead, Sir Ferdinand. Whats the latest?

SIR F. You know, I presume, that your father's money, now practically unlimited, has been made, and is still being made, on the money market, by buying stocks and shares and selling them again at a profit. Such profits are not taxed, as they are classed as capital, not as income. Consequently it has been possible for your father to remain enormously rich, although the war taxation has abolished rich men as a class.

THE YOUTH. So much the better for us.

SIR F. Not altogether. The Chancellor of the Exchequer may tax money market incomes, either as such or as gambling. In that case The Buoyant Billions will dry up abruptly. In any case they will stop with his death, which cannot now be far off. Your incomes will be taxed like everyone elses, if you have any incomes. Have you?

THE WIDOWER. All I know is that what money I need appears to my credit in my bank passbook as cash or dividends on the few investments my stockbroker has advised.

SIR F. Does that apply all round?

SECONDBORN. To me, yes.

DARKIE. I told you so, Sir Ferdinand. None of us knows anything about making money because our father knows all about it.

SIR F. Has he never taught you anything about it?

THE WIDOWER. He couldnt. He does not understand it himself. He makes money by instinct, as beavers build dams.

SECONDBORN. Whenever I have taken his financial advice I have lost by it. I now leave it to my banker.

SIR F. Then I am afraid I must warn you all that you will presently become very poor. You will have to let your country houses and live in gate lodges and gardeners' cottages. Your ladies will have to do the housework. Your clothes will have to last you for years. I am here to impress these hard facts on you.

THE WIDOWER. But surely this shortage will not last for ever. The Labor Government, which is responsible for these robberies of the rich, will be defeated at the next election.

SIR F. Do not depend on that. All the king's horses and all the king's men cannot bring back the unearned incomes of the nineteenth century. The Socialists and Trade Unionists will see to that.

DARKIE. None of us women knows how to do housework.

SIR F. I am afraid you will have to learn.

MRS SECONDBORN. The whole thing is utterly ridiculous. The war is over; and there will always be rich and poor. The Chancellor is a beggar on horseback. He will be sent back to the gutter at the next election.

SIR F. Nobody can object to these revolutionary changes more than I do; but they are occurring among my clients every day.

MRS SECONDBORN. Nonsense! We must live. What are we to do?

SIR F. Reduce your expenditure. Live as poorer people than yourselves now live.

MRS SECONDBORN. Oh yes, poor people. But we are not poor people. We cannot live that way.

MRS THIRDBORN. Why not? Our riches have not made us happy. Our Lord's mother was the wife of a carpenter. I have always thought of her as a woman who did her own housework. I am sure I could learn. Is it not easier for a camel to pass through the eye of a needle than for a rich woman to enter the kingdom of heaven?

MRS SECONDBORN. Oh, you are religious. Much good your religion will do us!

THE WIDOWER. Dont let us quarrel about religion.

THE YOUTH. The old man isnt dead yet. He will make billions, taxes or no taxes. Lets make the most of him while he lasts.

SECONDBORN. I find it hard to believe that he will ever die. He is a human calculating machine. Calculating machines dont die.

SIR F. They wear out. He cannot live for ever.

THE WIDOWER. I used to play the cornet fairly well. If only my wife were alive to play my accompaniments on a street piano I should not starve.

SIR F. None of you need starve. On your father's reputation you will live on company directorships. You need not know anything about the businesses; your name on the prospectus will be sufficient. I must now pass on to another matter. Mr Buoyant has added to his instruction this sentence. "My elder daughter is provided for and need not be present. She can take care of herself." Have you a sister, Miss Buoyant?

DARKIE. I have a stepsister.

SIR F. [*surprised*] Was your father twice married?

THE WIDOWER. He was; but we try to forget it. We are ashamed of it.

MRS THIRDBORN. I am not ashamed of it.

MRS SECONDBORN. Thats only your religion: you have no natural feelings. Of course we are ashamed of it.

SIR F. May I ask what was wrong about it?

THE WIDOWER. Nothing wrong. But when our father married he was a very poor man; and he married a very

31

common woman. She had never in her life had a satisfying dinner; and she died of overeating when they could afford it. They had one daughter.

MRS SECONDBORN. A quite impossible person.

SIR F. In what way?

DARKIE. She can do everything we cant do. She can cook. She can make beds. She can make her own clothes. She can sweep and scrub. She can nurse. She learnt it all before she was ten, and was sent to a ladies' school.

MRS SECONDBORN. Nothing could make a real lady of her. She dresses like a lady, and can talk like a lady, and can behave like a lady when she likes; but she does not belong to us. Her ten years of poverty and commonness makes a difference we cannot get over. She knows things a lady ought not to know.

MRS THIRDBORN. Including some things nobody ought to know. But it is not her fault.

MRS SECONDBORN. She has no manners at home, and no education. She keeps them for visitors. No class.

SIR F. My dear good people, you are behind the times. It is now a disgrace to have been born rich. Fashion is led by the wives of Cabinet Ministers whose fathers and husbands began on five shillings a week: they boast of it. Your stepsister is probably ashamed of you. May I ask where she is at present?

THE WIDOWER. In Panama, we believe.

SIR F. Panama!

THE YOUTH. On the banks of the canal all alone in a shack put up by herself and a few natives.

SECONDBORN. An interesting experience. When I feel that I can no longer bear civilized society I retreat into pure mathematics. But I need not go to Panama for that, thank Heaven.

MRS SECONDBORN. No: because I provide a comfortable home for you, where you can see whom you like when you like. This woman lives like a savage in a swamp full of snakes and alligators and natives.

SECONDBORN. My dear: the world is so wicked and ignorant and unreasonable that I must get away from it occasionally.

MRS SECONDBORN. You do it to get away from me. You think I dont know; but I do. Am I wicked and ignorant and unreasonable?

SECONDBORN. Occasionally, my dear. Only occasionally. Not always.

MRS SECONDBORN. Well, of all the monstrous accusations—

SIR F. Need we go into your domestic affairs? We really must not be personal.

MRS SECONDBORN. Whatever is not personal is not human.

The woman from Panama dashes into the temple, in travelling dress, and in a blazing rage.

SHE. What is all this? Why was I not told? [*To Sir F.*] Who are you?

SIR F. I am Mr Buoyant's solicitor, in consultation with his family. May I ask whom I am addressing?

SHE. You are addressing old Bill Buoyant's firstborn, next to himself the head of the family.

SIR F. Then you are expressly excluded from this family council on the ground that you are already provided for. The rest may have to face ruin when your father dies.

SHE. Well, here I am and here I stay. When they are all ruined they will expect me to keep them on my annuity. I cant and wont. So now give me a chair.

THE YOUTH [*giving her his chair*] Here you are, Clemmy. [*He plants it in front of the altar at the side opposite to Sir Ferdinand; fetches another for himself; and resumes his place*].

SIR F. Did you say Clemmy? The name in my instructions is Babzy.

SHE. Babzy is my vulgar father's vulgar pet name for his vulgar first baby. I was christened Clementina Alexandra; but Babzy is shorter: my father would not change it. Clemmy to the others.

MRS SECONDBORN. Have you come home for good?

33

SHE. That wont matter to you, Julia. For my home is here, in Daddy's house, not in yours. Daddy is growing old; and old men sometimes do foolish things with their money. None of you knows anything about money; so I had better keep an eye on you and him. Where is Daddy?

SIR F. Mr Buoyant is staying away purposely. He has no gift of expression; and his children, he tells me, are too much for him as talkers, and generally arrive at wrong conclusions by talking their feet off the ground. I am quoting his own words. Having done my best to act for him without making the least impression on your very interesting relatives, I really do not know why I am staying, especially as you appear to be taking my place. I had better go.

SHE. No. Stay for the fun of it. Whats your name, by the way?

SIR F. Envelopes should be addressed to Sir Ferdinand Flopper, Bart.

SHE. What! The great Sir Ferdinand?

SIR F. You are good enough to put it that way. Now may I ask you a question?

SHE. Ask a dozen if you like.

SIR F. You did not come back from Panama to attend this meeting. You must have left before it was decided on.

SHE. How clever of you to think of that! I came because I was attacked by the symptoms of a very dangerous disease.

They all shew great concern, exclaiming Oh *in their various ways.*

SIR F. Oh! You came for medical advice. I beg your pardon.

SHE. No. It's not a doctor's job. I found myself what is called falling in love. I had illusions, infatuations, impulses that were utterly unreasonable and irresistible. Desires in which my body was taking command of my soul. And all for a man of whom I knew nothing: a passing vagabond who had begged a meal from me. He came to me next day and said he had fallen in love with me at first sight, and that he was going quite mad about me. He warned me to run away and leave no address, as he would follow me to the ends of the earth if he knew where I was; and we should both make fools of ourselves by getting married. So I fled; and here I am. He does not know my name, nor I his. But when I think of him everything is transfigured and I am magically happy. Unreadable poems like the Song of Solomon delight me: bagatelles by Beethoven deepen into great sonatas: every walk through the country is an exploration of the plains of heaven. My reason tells me that this cannot possibly be real; that the day will come when it will vanish and leave me face to face with reality; perhaps tied to a husband who may be anything from a criminal to an intolerable bore. So I have run away and put the seas between me and this figure that looks like a beautiful and wonderful celestial messenger —a Lohengrin—but really does not exist at all except in my imagination. So now you know, all of you. Let us change the subject.

SIR F. Not, if you please, until I have reminded you that very few men are criminals, and that most married couples spend the whole day apart, the woman in the house, the man in the office or study or workshop. And there is such a possibility as divorce.

THE WIDOWER. Besides, take my case. My late wife and I were so indispensable to oneanother that a separation would have been for us a desolating calamity. Yet I repeatedly found myself irresistibly attracted biologically by females with whom I could not converse seriously for five minutes. My wife needed some romance in her life when I ceased to be romantic to her and became only her matter-of-fact husband. To keep her in good humor and health I had to invite and entertain a succession of interesting young men to keep her supplied with what I call Sunday husbands.

MRS SECONDBORN. That is a perfectly different thing. You have low tastes, which you occasionally gratify. I take an interest in young men; but I do not misconduct myself with them.

SECONDBORN. That, my love, is because your sense of property is stronger than your biological instinct. I am your property. Therefore you are damnably jealous.

MRS SECONDBORN. I deny it. I am not jealous.

THE WIDOWER. I think Sir Ferdinand's mind would be clearer on the subject if, like me, he had been married twice. My first marriage, which was quite biological, was a failure. What people called our love turned into something very like hatred. But biological tastes are not low tastes. Our two children were great successes: beautiful children with good characters. But nobody could live in the same house with their mother.

SIR F. [*very gravely*] Excuse me. I do not think you should speak of your dead wife in such terms.

THE WIDOWER. Oh, she is not dead: I let her divorce me. We are now quite good friends again. But to understand this question it is not enough to have been married once. Henry the Eighth would be the leading authority if he were alive. The prophet Mahomet was married more than fourteen times. And what about Solomon?

SIR F. Do pray let us keep religion out of this discussion. Surely religion is one thing, and the British marriage law another.

All the rest laugh, except Mrs Secondborn, who snorts.

SIR F. What is there to laugh at? Can we not be sensible and practical? We are dealing with the hard cash of your incomes, not with Solomon and Mahomet. We are not Mormons. Their wives in British law were only concubines.

THE WIDOWER. I hold that concubines are a necessary institution. In a nation wellbred biologically there should be concubines as well as wives and husbands. Some marriages are between couples who have no children because they have hereditary ailments which they fear to transmit to their offspring. Others are of shrews and bullies who produce excellent bastards, though domestic life with them is impossible. They should be concubines, not husbands and wives. All concubinages are exactly alike. No two marriages are alike.

SIR F. Nonsense! All marriages are exactly alike in law.

THE WIDOWER. So much the worse for law, I am afraid.

MRS THIRDBORN. No two love affairs are alike. I was in love three times before I married a friend who was not in love with me nor I with him. We were both sane. Yet we can say honestly "Whom God hath joined"—

SIR F. Oh, do please leave God out of the question. Marriage is a legal institution; and God has nothing to do with legal institutions.

MRS THIRDBORN. God keeps butting in somehow.

SIR F. Surely that is not the way to speak of the Almighty. If you must drag in religion, at least do so in becoming language.

MRS THIRDBORN. When you really believe in God you can make fun of Him. When you are only pretending you pull long faces and call Him Gawd.

MRS SECONDBORN. Dont forget that when you wake up from your dreams and delusions about your husband you have your children to love. You may be only too glad to be rid of your crazy notions about your husband. The kids fill his place.

MRS THIRDBORN. Not after they are six, when they go to school and begin to be independent of you and form a new relation with their teachers. Only husband and wife come to feel that they belong to oneanother and are really parts of oneanother. That is one of the mysteries of marriage.

MRS SECONDBORN. Besides, the illusions dont affect people who have common sense. I never read the Song of Solomon, nor bothered about Beethoven; but I always knew whether it was a fine day or a wet one without any nonsense about the plains of heaven. Dick's weaknesses were as obvious to me then as they are now. But I could put up with them. I liked him because he was so unlike me. [*To her husband*] And it was the same with you, wasn't it, Dick?

SECONDBORN. Not quite. I had my share of the illusions. But when they vanished they did not matter much. I had got used to you. Let us look at this mathematically. The sex illusion is not a fixed quantity: not what mathematicians call a constant. It varies from zero in my wife's case to madness in that of our stepsister. Reason and experience, which hold it in check, are also variable. Our stepsister is highly observant and reasonable. My wife is totally unreasonable.

MRS SECONDBORN. Which of us two is the reasonable one? Who keeps the house for you? Who looks after your clothes? Who sees that you get your meals regularly and

37

do not eat and drink more than is good for you? Reason! I have to reason with you every day, and can get nothing out of you but incomprehensible ravings about variables and functions. Your mind never stays put for ten minutes at a time.

SECONDBORN. My dearest: nothing in the world ever stays put for ten seconds. We can know it only relatively at any moment. Yet most people can think only absolutely. Relatively, variably, mathematically, they cannot think at all. Everything for them is either soot or whitewash. They undertake to make a new world after every war without brains enough to add *a* to *b*.

MRS SECONDBORN. Are you happy with me or are you not?

SECONDBORN. I am never happy. I dont want to be happy. I want to be alive and active. Bothering about happiness is the worst unhappiness.

DARKIE. Oh, let us talk sense. [*To her stepsister*] Clemmy: your room is not ready for you: to clear it will take weeks. And there are no maids to be got now.

SHE. English maids are no use to me. I have brought a Panama native: he will clear my room for me in twenty minutes.

THE WIDOWER. Then our business is finished. Sir Ferdinand has told us that our incomes will stop when our father dies. He has advised us that we can live on directorships on the strength of our famous name and its associations with billions. I hope so. What more is there to be said?

THE YOUTH. What about me? Nobody will make me a director. I am a world betterer.

SIR F. World betterer! What new hare are you starting now?

THE YOUTH. All intelligent men of my age are world betterers today.

SIR F. Pooh! You will drop all that nonsense when you take your university degree.

THE WIDOWER. Impossible. Our father gave us all the money we needed on condition that we would never engage in money making, nor take a university degree.

SIR F. Not go to a university!

SECONDBORN. You misunderstand. We have all spent three years at college. Our father sent us there to acquire the social training the communal life of a university gives. But he insisted on our leaving without a degree.

SIR F. In Heaven's name, why?

SECONDBORN. One of his notions. He holds that dictated mental work on uncongenial subjects is overwork which injures the brain permanently. So we are not university graduates; but we are university men none the less. If a man is known to have been at Oxford or Cambridge nobody ever asks whether he has taken a degree or not.

SIR F. But that does not justify false pretences.

THE YOUTH. University degrees are the falsest of pretences. Graduates as a class are politically and scientifically obsolete and ignorant. Even in the elementary schools children spend nine years without learning how to speak their native language decently or write it easily.

THE WIDOWER. We are not impostors, Sir Ferdinand, because we ran away from our examinations. What culture a university can give, we possess. However, if you have any scruples—

SIR F. I have scruples. I have principles. I have common sense. I have sanity. They seem to have no place in the affairs of this family.

MRS THIRDBORN. Listen to me, Sir Ferdinand. You must understand that my father-in-law's dearest wish was to be a teacher and a preacher. But as he had original ideas no one would employ him as a preacher nor listen to him as a teacher. He could do nothing but make money: though he regarded it as the curse of his life. He made it in the city all day and returned to his home every evening to forget it, and teach his children to speak their minds always and never to mistake saying the proper thing for the truth.

SIR F. But surely the truth is always the proper thing.

MRS THIRDBORN. Yes; but the proper thing is not always God's truth.

SIR F. [*bothered*] You give things such a twist! We really shall get nowhere unless you will speak in an expected manner.

The Panama native, attired as a British valet, enters hastily and comes straight to Her.

NATIVE. Pink lady: the man has come.

SHE. Here!!!

NATIVE. In this house. He will not be denied. He has divine guidance. He has seen you again at the singing theatre here in London. God led him to Panama.

SHE. Shew him up.

The Native bows his assent and goes out.

SIR F. May I ask who is this man?

SHE. He is the man I am in love with: the object of my illusions, my madness. If he followed me across the Atlantic, and tracked me back again, he must be as mad as I am.

NATIVE [*at the door, announcing*] The man of destiny. [*He withdraws*].

The Son, elegantly dressed, enters.

HE [*to Her, standing in the middle of the temple after looking at the company in dismay*] Am I intruding? I had hoped to find you alone.

SHE. The Buoyants are never alone. Let me introduce you. My stepbrothers, Tom and Dick. Mrs Dick and Mrs Harry: a grass widow. Tom is a widower. Darkie: my unmarried stepsister. Fiffy: the youngest. Sir Ferdinand Whopper, our father's latest and most eminent solicitor.

SIR F. My name is not Whopper: it is Flopper.

SHE. My mistake. They rhyme.

HE. Bon soir la compagnie. This room is like a temple. Are you engaged in an act of worship?

MRS THIRDBORN. All the world is a temple of the Holy Ghost. You may be quite at your ease here, resting your soul.

SIR F. In what capacity do you claim to join us, may I ask?

HE. Only in pursuit of old Bill Buoyant's billions. I am by profession a world betterer. I need money for investigation and experiment. I saw Miss Buoyant one night at the

40

opera. She attracted me so strongly that I did not hear a
note of the music. I found out who she was but not what she
is. I know nothing of her tastes, her intelligence, her manners, her temper: in short, of anything that would make it
possible for me to live with her; yet I feel that I must possess her. For this I have no excuse. Nature has struck this
blow at me: I can neither explain it nor resist it: I am mad
about her. All I can do is to marry her for her money if I
can persuade her to marry me.

SIR F. Do I understand that you propose to marry this
lady for her money, and are apologizing for wanting to
marry her for love as well?

HE. I said nothing about love. Love means many different things: love of parents and children, love of pet animals, love of whisky or strawberry ices, love of cricket or
lawn tennis, also love of money. My case is a specific one of
animal magnetism, as inexplicable as the terrestrial magnetism that drags a steel ship to a north or south pole that
is not the astronomical pole. The ship can be demagnetized:
who can demagnetize me? No one. We have not even a
name for this mystery.

SIR F. I should call it the voice of nature.

HE. How much farther does that get you? Calling
things names does not explain them: it is the trade of sham
scientists who do not know what science means.

SECONDBORN. That is true. Are you a mathematician?

HE. I know the multiplication table, and can do very
simple sums: that is all; but though I cannot do equations,
I am mathematician enough to know that nothing is sta-
tionary: everything is moving and changing.

SHE. What complicates the affair is that I am in love
with this man. And I dare not marry a man I love. I should
be his slave.

SIR F. Really you are all quite mad. Is not your being in
love with him a reason for marrying him if he is in love
with you, as he appears to be in spite of his outrageous boast
of being a fortune hunter?

SHE. You may leave money out of the question. Though
I was brought up never to think of money, I have never

spent all my annuity; and with what I could spare I have doubled my income on the money market. I have inherited my father's flair for finance. Money makes itself in my hands in spite of his preaching. When I want a husband I can afford to pay for him.

HE. That is very satisfactory. Why not marry me?

SHE. We might regret it. Love marriages are the most unreasonable, and probably the most often regretted.

HE. Everything we do can be regretted. There is only one thing that a woman is certain to regret.

SHE. What is that, pray?

HE. Being unmarried.

SHE. I deny it. The day of ridiculous old maids is over. Great men have been bachelors and great women virgins.

HE. They may have regretted it all the same.

SIR F. I must remind you, Miss Buoyant, that though many women have regretted their marriages there is one experience that no woman has ever regretted, and that experience is motherhood. Celibacy for a woman is *il gran rifiuto*, the great refusal of her destiny, of the purpose in life which comes before all personal considerations: the replacing of the dead by the living.

MRS THIRDBORN. For once, dear Sir Ferdinand, you are not talking nonsense. Child bearing is an experience which it is impossible to regret. It is definitely ordained.

SECONDBORN. Regret is essentially mathematical. What are the mathematical probabilities? How many marriages are regretted? How much are they regretted? How long are they regretted? What is the proportion of divorces? The registrar of marriages should have a totalizator balancing these quantities. There should be one in every church. People would then know what chances they are taking. Should first cousins marry? Should Catholics and Protestants marry? Should lepers marry? At what ages should they marry? Without these statistics you cannot give scientific answers to these questions: you have only notions and guesswork to go on.

HE. Our fancies come first: they are irresistible. They must have a meaning and a purpose. Well, I have a strong

42

fancy for your stepsister; and she confesses to a strong fancy for me. Let us chance it.

DARKIE. What about your own experience, Sir Ferdinand?

SHE. Yes. How did your own marriage turn out? Did you marry for love?

SIR F. I am not married. I am a bachelor.

They laugh at him.

SIR F. What are you all laughing at? Am I expected to substitute personal experiences for legal advice? May I not advise women though I am not a woman? I am here to advise a family which I can only describe charitably as a family of lunatics. Does not the value of my advice lie in the fact that I am not myself a lunatic?

THE YOUTH. But you are a lunatic. And you havnt given us any advice.

SECONDBORN. What have you given us? Instead of facts, escapist romance from the cinemas. Instead of mathematical and relative measurements, a three dimensional timeless universe. Instead of logic, association of ideas, mostly nonsensical ideas. Instead of analysis, everything in totalitarian lumps. Nothing scientific.

SIR F. I am a lawyer, not a scientist.

SECONDBORN. Until law and science, politics and religion, are all one, the scientists, the lawyers, the clergymen, the politicians will be foolish tinkers who think they can mend the world because they can mend holes in a saucepan.

DARKIE. Do let us get back to tin tacks. Is Clemmy going to marry him or is she not? If she says yes I bet she will have her own way whatever he does.

THE WIDOWER. The woman always does. I have gone twice to my weddings like a lamb to the slaughter house. My two wives were triumphant. I bought new clothes, oiled and brushed my hair, and was afraid to run away. My second marriage was a success: I knew what to expect. Second marriages are the quietest and happiest. The twice married, if one of them dies, marry a third time even at the most advanced age.

SIR F. Then marriage is not a failure as an institution.

43

With reasonable divorce laws, not at all.

HE [*to Her*] You hear?

SHE. Sit down, will you. Dont stand over me, pontificating.

HE. I beg your pardon. [*He sits down on the altar step in the middle*].

SHE. You make everything beautiful to me. You give me a happiness I have never experienced before. But if I marry you all this will cease. If I dont marry you—if you die—if we never meet again, it may last all my life. And there are rights I will give to no man over me.

SIR F. Conjugal rights. They cannot now be enforced. Not effectively. Do not let them hinder you. What are the gentleman's means? that is the question.

SHE. What am I to do with my means? that also is the question.

HE. What all independent women do with their means. Keep a husband on them.

MRS SECONDBORN. Is a husband a dog or a cat to be kept as a pet? I never heard such nonsense.

HE. Dogs are sometimes better bargains. I am not so sure about cats.

MRS SECONDBORN [*rising*] Come home, Dick. I have had enough of this. It will just end in their getting married like other people. Come home. [*She storms out*].

MRS THIRDBORN [*rising*] Sir Ferdinand's law has failed us. Dick's science has failed us. Fiff's boyish dreams have failed us: he has not yet bettered the world. We must leave it in God's hands. [*She goes out*].

SECONDBORN [*rising*] It always comes to that: leave it to God, though we do not know what God is, and are still seeking a general mathematical theory expressing Him. All we know is that He leaves much of it to us; and we make a shocking mess of it. We must be goodnatured and make the best of it. Goodbye, Mr Golddigger. [*He follows his wife out*].

THE WIDOWER [*rising*] As I have no wife to decide for me, I must go of my own accord.

SIR F. [*rising*] As nobody pays the slightest attention to

my advice, I will accompany you. [*The three go out*].

DARKIE [*rising*] Come on, Fiff. Lets leave them alone together.

HE. Thank you.

Darkie and Fiff go out.

HE. Well?

SHE. I will think about it.

The Chinese Priest returns, followed by the Native swinging a censer.

THE PRIEST. Will you have the kindness to follow your friends and leave me to purify this temple of peace. It has been terribly profaned for the last hour. Father Buoyant will be here presently for his rest, his meditation, his soothing, his divine recreation. You have poisoned its atmosphere with your wranglings. I must change its air and restore its peace lest it kill Father Buoyant instead of giving him a foretaste of heaven. Go now: you must not breathe here any longer.

SHE [*rising*] Daddy made me sit still and be silent here when I was in my restless teens. I detested it. The scent of incense sickens me. [*To Him*] Come, you. We must think it over.

She goes out. He waves his hand to the Priest and follows.

THE PRIEST. What freaks these pinks are! Belonging neither to the west, like you, nor to the east, like me.

THE NATIVE [*swinging the censer*] Neither to the north nor south; but in that they resemble us. They have much to teach us.

THE PRIEST. Yes; but they are themselves unteachable, not understanding what they teach.

THE NATIVE. True: they can teach; but they cannot learn.

THE PRIEST. Freaks. Dangerous freaks. The future is with the learners.

The temple vanishes, blacked out.

45

ACT IV
THE END

WHEN *the temple reappears the censer is on the altar. The Priest and the Native are rearranging the chairs.*

Old Bill Buoyant comes in. A greybeard, like any other greybeard; but a gorgeous golden dressing gown and yellow slippers give him a hieratic air.

OLD BILL. Have they all cleared out?

PRIEST. All. The temple is cleansed.

OLD BILL. Good. Who is your friend?

NATIVE. I am the servant of your daughter.

OLD BILL. Which daughter?

NATIVE. From Panama.

OLD BILL. Good. Has she left the house yet?

NATIVE. Not without me. I drive her car.

OLD BILL. Good. Tell her to come and see me here.

NATIVE. At your service, O sage. [*He salaams and goes out*].

OLD BILL. Shall I profane the temple if I kiss my daughter here? I am fond of her.

PRIEST. Truly no. The temple will sanctify your kiss.

OLD BILL. Good. It is curious how happy I always feel here. I am not a religious man. I do not go to church.

PRIEST. You meditate.

OLD BILL. No. Meditation is not in my line: I speculate. And my speculations turn out well when I spend an hour here and just empty my mind.

PRIEST. When the mind is empty the gods take possession. And the gods know.

OLD BILL. Yes: I suppose thats it. But it's a queer business: I thought I was the very last man in the world to put my nose into a temple. However, you know all this. I am repeating myself, and boring you. Leave me to myself. [*He seats himself in the bishop's chair*].

PRIEST. I repeat the service every day; yet it does not bore me: there is always something new in it. They tell me it is the same with your orchestral symphonies: the great

46

ones cannot be heard too often. But as you desire, I leave you to your aftercalm.

OLD BILL. So long, Mahatma.

The Priest nods gravely, and is going when She and He come in.

THE PRIEST. Peace be with you three. [*He goes*].

SHE [*rushing to Old Bill and kissing him*] Daddyest!

OLD BILL [*returning her embrace*] My Babzy! Who is the man?

SHE. I dont know. He wants to marry me.

OLD BILL. Does he indeed? Do you want to marry him?

SHE. I am considering it. I am not dead set against it.

OLD BILL. Whats his name?

SHE. I dont know.

OLD BILL. The devil you dont!

SHE [*to Him*] Whats your name?

HE. Smith. Only Smith. Christened Junius.

OLD BILL. Have you nothing else to say for yourself?

JUNIUS. Nothing whatever.

OLD BILL. Any profession?

HE. World betterer. Nothing paying.

SHE. If I marry him I shall have to keep him and manage for him. But that is not altogether a drawback. I do not mean to be any man's kept slave.

OLD BILL [*to Junius*] What about you? Do you want to be any woman's kept man?

JUNIUS. I dont want anything but your daughter. I dont know why. I know nothing about her; and she knows nothing about me. I am simply mad on the subject.

OLD BILL [*to Her*] Are you mad on the subject?

SHE. Not so mad as he is. I can do without him. If not, I should be his slave.

OLD BILL. Do you hear that, young man? You will be the slave.

JUNIUS. I suppose so. But I must risk it. So must she. You can understand this. You have made your billions by taking risks.

OLD BILL. I have seen men ruined by taking risks. I have a sort of instinct about them which brings me out all right.

For old Bill Buoyant there are no risks. But for you, perhaps???

JUNIUS. Well, there may be none for your daughter.
She may inherit your genius.

OLD BILL. She does. But my genius tells me not to throw
away my daughter on a young lunatic.

JUNIUS. You are jealous, eh? Let me remind you that
all parents must see their children walk out sooner or
later. Mothers-in-law are stock jokes. Nobody jokes about
fathers-in-law; but they are troublesome enough when
they hold on too long.

SHE. Parents cannot be turned out into the woods to die.
We are not savages. Daddy will always be a part of my life.

JUNIUS. Not always. How long do you intend to live,
old man?

OLD BILL. Not for ever: God forbid! [*To Her*] The
fellow is right, darling. Leave me out of the question.

SHE. I cant leave you out, Daddy. But you will know
your natural place in my house: you have always known it
in your own. I can trust you.

JUNIUS. I have no objection to your father as long as he
lasts. He has the billions.

OLD BILL. The billions will stop when I die. Would you
be as keen if there were no billions?

JUNIUS. Just as keen. How often must I tell you that
I am mad about her? But we shall want the money. I have
earned nothing so far.

OLD BILL [*to Her*] He has an eye for facts, this chap. I
rather like him.

SHE. Yes: so do I. He has no illusions about himself nor
about me. After all, if he turns out badly I can divorce him.

OLD BILL. Well, our parting must come someday; and
if you and I were the wisest father and daughter on earth
the upshot would be just as much a toss-up as if we were
the two damndest fools. Still, there are certain precautions
one can take.

JUNIUS. A joint annuity, for instance.

OLD BILL. Your sense of money is very clear, young man.
But I have already bought her an annuity for her life. Not

48

for yours. Any further precautions you must take yourself.

JUNIUS. I must agree. The Life Force has got me. I can make no conditions.

OLD BILL [to Her] Well, will you marry him?

SHE. I will consider it.

JUNIUS. If you consider it you will refuse. There would be no marriages if the two started considering.

OLD BILL. That is the first stupid thing you have said, young man. All marriages are very anxiously considered; but considering has never yet prevented a marriage. If you are her man she will have you, consideration or no consideration.

SHE. What do you advise, Daddy?

OLD BILL. Oh, take him, take him. I like him; and he will do as well as another. You may regret it; but you will regret it worse if you are afraid to try your luck.

JUNIUS. I am surprised and deeply obliged to you, Mr Buoyant. I expected you to use all your influence against me. You are a model father-in-law.

SHE. I feel as if I were going to commit suicide.

JUNIUS. In a sense, you are. So am I. The chrysalis dies when the dragonfly is born.

SHE. I am no chrysalis. I am a working bee: you are a drone.

JUNIUS. That is nature's arrangement. We cannot change it.

OLD BILL. A working husband is no husband at all. When I had to work, my wife was only my housekeeper: she saw next to nothing of me except when I came home at night hungry and tired and dirty. When I did nothing but send telegrams to my stockbroker—I dont call that work—and buy fancy waistcoats and diamond cravat pins, she began to enjoy her marriage and love me. And long as she has been dead now, I have never been unfaithful to her, nor ever shall be.

JUNIUS. But you married again.

OLD BILL. It was not the same thing. I wanted more children because I was so fond of the one I had. But it was not the same.

JUNIUS. Did you never think of bettering the world with your money?

OLD BILL. What the devil do I care about the world? What did it care about me when I was poor? Dont talk your world bettering cant to me if we are to get on together. I am not going to buy any of your shares.

JUNIUS. I apologize. My shares pay no dividends. I will not pursue the subject. When are we to get married? Name the day.

OLD BILL. Dont frighten her. When she names it, you will be frightened.

JUNIUS. I am frightened already. But we must dare. By the way, where shall we live? Not in Panama, I hope.

SHE. No. In Panama I should be nervous about you when you were out of my sight. You cannot charm the rattlers and gaters as I can.

JUNIUS. Why not? I can learn the saxophone.

SHE. True; but we should be out of reach of Daddy. We shall live in Park Lane.

JUNIUS. You know, of course, that there are plenty of rattlers and gaters of the human variety in Park Lane?

SHE. Yes; and you may be one of them.

JUNIUS. You have an answer for everything. What a prospect for me!

SHE. We are both taking chances. We shall live where I like.

JUNIUS. Or where I like. I can assert myself.

SHE. So can I. We shall see which of us wins. Stop chattering; and go out and buy a marriage licence.

JUNIUS [*taken aback*] Oh, I say! This is very sudden.

OLD BILL. Frightened, eh? Go. Get it over. You will have to arrange for two witnesses.

JUNIUS. I wish I could arrange for an anesthetist. The operation is terrifying.

SHE. Dont forget to buy a wedding ring. Have you money enough?

JUNIUS. I have what is left of the thousand pounds my father started me with. Panama made a big hole in it.

OLD BILL. Off with you, damn you. You are stealing my

daughter from me. I hope she will soon tire of you and come back to me. [*To Her*] Give him one of your rings to get the fit right. Never mind the witnesses: Tom and Dick will do.

JUNIUS [*to Her*] Wouldnt you like to be married in church and have the banns called? That would give us three weeks to think it over.

SHE. No. Now or never.

JUNIUS. I am being rushed.

OLD BILL. You will spend your life being rushed if you live with Babz. Better get used to it at once.

SHE. A ring that will fit your middle finger will be big enough for my third. I have bigger hands. I was brought up to use them. You werent.

JUNIUS. You must put up with that. My hands are those of a philosopher: yours of a charwoman. Oh, why, WHY am I infatuated with you? I know so many apparently superior women.

SHE. Same here. Daddy is worth ten of you.

JUNIUS. You think so. But if you only knew how quickly I can lose money. He can only make it.

OLD BILL. Leave me out of it: I shall not last much longer: you have a lifetime to give her. Away with you to the registry office and stop talking.

JUNIUS. I go. But I'm not sure I shall ever come back. [*He goes out*].

SHE. I half hope he wont.

JUNIUS [*coming back*] By the way, whats your Christian name?

SHE. Clementina Alexandra.

JUNIUS. Righto! [*Making a note of it*] Cle-Men-Tina Alexandra. [*He goes*].

SHE [*throwing her arms round Old Bill's neck and kissing him*] Daddy! Daddy! Daddy!

The Native comes in and closes the door carefully. Babz quickly releases her father.

THE NATIVE [*to Her*] Sir Flopper, the illustrious law servant of God, has waited until your venerable father is disengaged. May he enter?

OLD BILL. Yes. Shew him in.

THE NATIVE [*looks to Her for confirmation*] ??

SHE. Yes. Shew him in.

THE NATIVE [*throwing the door open*] Enter, Excellency.

Sir Ferdinand comes in. The Native withdraws.

SIR FERDINAND [*to Old Bill*] Pardon. I thought you were alone.

OLD BILL. Get out, Babzy.

SHE. Au revoir, Sir Ferdinand.

He opens the door for her and bows gravely as she passes out, then closes the door, and, after an inviting gesture from Old Bill, sits down in the chair vacated by her.

SIR FERDINAND. First let me say that I am not here professionally.

OLD BILL. Why not? You must live.

SIR FERDINAND. My reason is that I am totally incapable of advising you on the subject of your extraordinary family. They are outside my experience. If I were a medical adviser I should certify them as insane.

OLD BILL. And me?

SIR FERDINAND. Well, hardly yet. Your instructions were rational enough. I put your financial case before your sons as you desired. I was interrupted by the arrival from America of the lady who has just left us. I was interrupted again by the arrival of a young man who proposed to marry her for her money. Your daughter made no objection: she seemed to prefer it to a disinterested proposal. Your family did not demur. I am prepared to learn that you do not demur. In any other family he would have been kicked out of the house.

OLD BILL. I like the fellow.

SIR FERDINAND. Like the fellow! Like an impudent fortune hunter! In Heaven's name, why?

OLD BILL. He asks straight questions and gives straight answers. So does my daughter. I taught her to do it. It was all I could teach her. Didnt you notice it?

SIR FERDINAND. I did indeed. And I have come to tell you I can no longer act as your solicitor. My brother Cyril is a doctor, head of a mental hospital for incurables. He is the man you should consult. Lawyers are useless here.

OLD BILL. Come, come, Flopper! You know as well as I do that people who marry for money are happy together as often as other people. It is the love matches that break down because Providence wants sound children and does not care a snap of its fingers whether the parents are happy or not. It makes them mad about one another until the children are born, and then drops them like hot potatoes. Money guarantees comfort and what you call culture. Love guarantees nothing. I know this. You know it. My daughter knows it. The young man knows it. Are we mad because we act and speak accordingly? Are you sane because you pretend to be shocked by it? It is you who should go to the mental hospital.

SIR FERDINAND. That also is a matter for medical, not legal opinion. I will not discuss it. I have only to tell you that I explained to your second family as you instructed me, that the source of their incomes would dry up at your death, and they must then fend for themselves.

OLD BILL. Good. What did they say to that?

SIR FERDINAND. Nothing. I had to suggest that they should live by directorships founded on your reputation.

OLD BILL. Guinea pigs. No use: that game is up. The new Labor Government gives such jobs to superannuated Trade Union secretaries.

SIR FERDINAND. Then why have you not provided for your second family as you did for your first daughter?

OLD BILL. It is not the same. They dont belong to me as she does.

SIR FERDINAND. They will starve.

OLD BILL. No they wont. They can live on their wives' income. I took care of that.

SIR FERDINAND. Well, that is all I have to say. I shall accept no fees for it; but I shall be glad to keep up our acquaintance, if that will be agreeable to you.

OLD BILL. Why?

SIR FERDINAND. Pure curiosity.

OLD BILL. I dont believe you.

53

SIR FERDINAND [*rising, offended*] Do you accuse me of lying?

OLD BILL. Yes. There must be some attraction. Which woman is it? One of my sons' wives, eh?

SIR FERDINAND [*sitting down again, deflated*] Well, really! No: they are married women. You have two unmarried daughters.

OLD BILL. Darkie? I actually forgot Darkie. Think of that!

SIR FERDINAND. Do not misunderstand me. I am a bachelor, not a libertine. I want a daughter.

OLD BILL. Good. Ive always had an uneasy conscience about Darkie. Ive never been able to give her the affection Ive heaped on Babzy. She has never had a father. Take her; and be a father to her. Come as often as you please: you are one of the family now.

SIR FERDINAND. You take my breath away. This is too sudden. A minute ago I did not know why I wanted to keep on terms with you all. You have shoved it down my throat.

OLD BILL. That is the Buoyant way: it saves a lot of time. Now that you know, you had better stay to lunch.

SIR FERDINAND. No. I must go home and think it over. Never fear: I shall not back out.

Darkie comes in.

OLD BILL. Here she is. Telepathy. It runs in the family.

DARKIE. Oh! I beg your pardon. I did not know you were engaged. It is only to ask whether you will have asparagus or broad beans for lunch.

OLD BILL. Sparrowgrass? Yes: plenty of it. [*She turns to go*]. Wait a bit. Sir Ferdinand Flopper here has fallen for you. He wants to be your father.

DARKIE. I dont want a father. Ive never had a real father: I'm not accustomed to it. I'm only a housekeeper.

OLD BILL. Well, my child, you can have a real father now, a baronet. Try him. You can drop him if he doesnt suit. Somebody to spoil you as Ive spoilt Babzy.

DARKIE. I dont want to be spoilt. I like housekeeping; and I'm not sentimental. If I ever want to be spoilt I shall get married. I am sorry to disappoint you, Sir Ferdinand; but daughtering is a game I have no turn for.

SIR FERDINAND. I see. But at least youll not mind my keeping up my acquaintance with the family.

DARKIE. Not a bit. Let me know what you like to eat and drink: that is all. I must go now to see about father's lunch. Tata.

She goes out.

OLD BILL. Dumbfounded, eh?

SIR FERDINAND. Completely. What a house this is! She was not a bit surprised, though she was quite unprepared.

OLD BILL. We Buoyants are always prepared for the worst.

SIR FERDINAND. Or the best, I hope. My offer is hardly a misfortune, as I see it.

OLD BILL. It isnt. Dont fancy you have escaped her. She asked about your grub. She is glad to have one more to housekeep for. You may consider yourself adopted.

SIR FERDINAND. I am past considering anything.

OLD BILL. Youll get used to it.

SIR FERDINAND. Yes: I suppose I shall. The curious thing is, I am beginning to like it.

OLD BILL. Good. [*Looking at his watch*] I wonder whether that chap is coming back. He ought to be here by now.

The Widower enters.

THE WIDOWER. Look here, Ee Pee: the young man from Panama says he is going to be married to Clemmy. He wants me and Dick to be witnesses. Is that all right?

OLD BILL. Yes. Quite all right. Has he got the licence?

THE WIDOWER. Yes. And he has borrowed my wife's wedding ring for the ceremony. He was short of pocket money for a new one. The money for the licence cleaned him out.

OLD BILL. Then he has come back?

THE WIDOWER. Yes. A bit upset, naturally; but he means business.

OLD BILL. Good.

SIR FERDINAND. Excuse me; but what does Ee Pee mean? Esteemed Parent?

55

OLD BILL. No. Earthly Providence. Darkie's invention.

SIR FERDINAND. Ah! Precisely.

The youth Fiffy comes in.

FIFFY. Look here, Ee Pee. Clemmy and the man from Panama are going to marry. He has got the licence.

OLD BILL. Well, what is that to you, you young rip?

FIFFY. Only that the chap is a World Betterer. I thought you had enough of that from me.

OLD BILL. So I have. The pair of you want to better the world when you dont know enough of it to manage a fish and chips business.

FIFFY. True, O king. But we are needed in the world bettering business, not in fish and chips. Still, one World Betterer is enough in one family.

OLD BILL. Keep out of it then, you. You were born to talk and say nothing, to write and do nothing. That pays.

FIFFY. To make sure, I shall marry for money, as the Panama chap is doing. Dont you agree, Sir Ferdinand?

SIR FERDINAND. Yes, if you can find the lady. Dress better; and oil your hair.

Babzy comes back with her two stepsisters-in-law.

SHE. Dick, dear: shall I marry the man from Panama?

SECONDBORN. My dearest Clemmy: I cannot advise you. You must take chances; but they are not calculable mathematically. We have no figures to go on: the proportion of happy love marriages to happy marriages of convenience has never been counted.

MRS SECONDBORN. Do stop talking heartless nonsense, Dick. Has the man any means or expectations? Is he a gentleman? He speaks like a gentleman. He dresses like a gentleman. But he has not the feelings of a gentleman. He says things that no gentleman would dream of saying. That is all we know about him. Dont marry him, Clemmy.

SECONDBORN. My dear: she must take chances or not marry at all.

MRS SECONDBORN. Oh, bother your chances! Chances! Chances! Chances! You are always talking about chances. Talk sense.

SECONDBORN. You tell me so almost every day, dear. I

took my chance when I married you. But I do not regret it. You are the stupidest woman on earth; but you are a part of my life.

MRS SECONDBORN. Well, ask Sir Ferdinand which of us is right. Clemmy has low tastes; but that is no reason why she should throw herself away on a nobody.

SIR FERDINAND. I do not think, Mr Buoyant, that you can treat this question altogether as a mathematical one. You must take account of feelings, passions, emotions, intuitions, instincts, as well as cold quantities and figures and logic.

SECONDBORN [*rising to the occasion eloquently*] And who dares say that mathematics and reasoning are not passions? Mathematic perception is the noblest of all the faculties! This cant about their being soulless, dead, inhuman mechanisms is contrary to the plainest facts of life and history. What has carried our minds farther than mathematical foresight? Who has done more for enlightenment and civilization than Giordano Bruno, Copernicus, Galileo, Newton, Descartes, Rutherford, Einstein, all of them far seeing guessers carried away by the passion for measuring truth and knowledge that possessed and drove them? Will you set above this great passion the vulgar concupiscences of Don Juan and Casanova, and the romance of Beatrice and Francesca, of Irish Deirdre, the greatest bores in literature, mere names incidentally immortalized by a few lines in a great poem?

MRS THIRDBORN. They had hearts, Dick.

SECONDBORN. Hearts! What are hearts without brains? You mean that they had glands: pituitary glands, adrenal glands, thyroid glands, pouring hormones into their blood. Do you suppose that there is no mathematical hormone? Our anatomists have not yet discovered it; but it is there, undiscovered and invisible, pouring into our brains, controlled by our enzymes and catalysts as surely as our appetites for beef and brandy. La Rochefoucauld told you two centuries ago that though the appetite we call love is in everybody's mouth very few have ever experienced it. God is not Love: Love is not Enough: the appetite for more truth, more knowledge, for measurement and precision, is far more universal: even the dullest fools have some glimmer of it. My wife here never tires of playing bridge and solving crossword puzzles as she tires of housekeeping. Her love for me is very variable: it turns to hate in its terrible reactions. Mathematical passion alone has no reaction: our pleasure in it promises a development in which life will be an intellectual ecstasy surpassing the ecstasies of saints. Think of that, Clara. Take your chance, Clemmy. Forgive my prolixity. Ive done.

He flings himself back into his chair.

MRS SECONDBORN [*humbled*] Well, Dick, I will say that you are wonderful when you speak your piece, though I never understand a word. You must be the greatest man in the family: you always make me feel like a fool. I am proud of you. I may lose my temper sometimes; but I never hate you.

Darkie comes in.

OLD BILL. Ah! there you are. Youve missed something.

DARKIE. No: Ive been listening at the door.

FIFFY. By George, Dick, you were splendid. World bettering be damned! I shall qualify as a doctor and look for that hormone.

Junius comes in with the licence in his hand.

JUNIUS. Well, Ive come back after all. Here is the licence. Ive got the witnesses. Is it yes or no?

SHE. I suppose I must take my chance. Yes.

DARKIE. What I want to know is how many of you are staying for lunch.

The curtain falls and ends the play.

FARFETCHED FABLES

LII

1948

PREFACE

AS I have now entered my 93rd year, my fans must not expect from me more than a few crumbs dropped from the literary loaves I distributed in my prime, plus a few speculations as to what may happen in the next million light years that are troubling me in the queer second wind that follows second childhood.

Being unable to put everything in the heavens above and on the earth beneath into every page I write, as some of my correspondents seem to expect, I have had to leave some scraps and shavings out; and now I gather up a few of them and present them in the childish form of Farfetched Fables. Philosophic treatises, however precise and lucid, are thrown away on readers who can enjoy and sometimes even understand parables, fairy tales, novels, poems, and prophecies. Proverbs are more memorable than catechisms and creeds. Fictions like The Prodigal Son, The Good Samaritan, The Pilgrim's Progress, and Gulliver's Travels, stick in minds impervious to the Epistles of Paul, the sermons of Bunyan, and the wisecracks of Koheleth and Ecclesiasticus. Hard workers who devour my plays cannot all tackle my prefaces without falling asleep almost at once.

The Panjandrums of literature will no doubt continue to assume that whoever can read anything can read everything, and that whoever can add two and two, bet on a horse, or play whist or bridge, can take in the tensor calculus. I know better, and can only hope that a batch of childish fables may stick in some heads that my graver performances overshoot.

THE NEW PSYCHOBIOLOGY

Nowadays biology is taking a new turn in my direction. What I called metabiology when I wrote The Doctor's Dilemma has made a step towards reality as psychobiology. The medical profession has split violently into psychotherapists and old-fashioned pill and bottle prescribers backed by surgeons practising on our living bodies as flesh plumbers and carpenters. When these surgeons find a tumor or a cancer they just cut it out. When your digestion or excretion goes wrong the bottlemen dose you with hydrochloric acid or chalk-and-opium ("the old mixture") as the case may be. When these treatments fail, or when they are impracticable, they tell you sympathetically that you must die; and die you do, unless you cure yourself or are cured by a disciple of Mrs Eddy practising Christian Science.

The more intelligent, observant, and open-minded apothecaries and Sawboneses, wakened up by an extraordinarily indelicate adventurer named Sigmund Freud, and by the able Scotch doctor Scott Haldane (J. B. S. Haldane's father), become more and more sceptical of the dogma that a healthy body insures a healthy mind (*mens sana in corpore sano*) and more and more inclined to believe that an unhealthy body is the result of a diseased mind. As I write, a treatise on Mental Abnormality by Dr Millais Culpin has just been published. It would have been impossible when I wrote The Doctor's Dilemma. In spite of its author's efforts to be impartial, it is convincing and converting as to his evident belief that the old mechanistic surgery and *materia medica* cost many lives.

AM I A PATHOLOGICAL CASE?

This leads my restlessly speculative mind further than Dr Culpin has ventured. Is literary genius a disease? Shakespear, Walter Scott, Alexandre Dumas, myself: are we all mental cases? Are we simply incorrigible liars? Are players impostors and hypocrites? Were the Bible Christians right when they disowned Bunyan because the incidents he described had never occurred nor the characters of whom he told such circumstantial tales ever existed? He pleaded that Jesus had taught by parables; but this made matters worse; for the Bibliolators never doubted that the Prodigal Son and the Good Samaritan were historical personages whose adventures had actually occurred. To them Bunyan's plea, classing the parables with Esop's Fables and the stories of Reynard the Fox, was a blasphemy. The first Freudians used to recite a string of words to their patients, asking what they suggested, and studying the reaction, until they wormed their way into the sufferer's sub-conscious mind, and unveiled some forgotten trouble that had been worrying him and upsetting his health. By bringing it to light they cured the patient.

FARFETCHED FABLES

When this Freudian technique was tried on me it failed because the words suggested always something fictitious. On the salt marshes of Norfolk I had been struck by the fact that when the horses stood round timidly at a distance, a handsome and intelligent donkey came and conversed with me after its fashion. I still have the photograph I took of this interesting acquaintance. The word Ass would have recalled this experience to any normal person. But when it was put to me, I immediately said Dogberry. I was once shewn the dagger with which Major Sirr killed Lord Edward Fitzgerald; but the word dagger got nothing from me but Macbeth. Highway or stile produced Autolycus, Interpreter the Pilgrim's Progress, blacksmith Joe Gargery. I was living in an imaginary world. Deeply as I was interested in politics, Hamlet and Falstaff were more alive to me than any living politician or even any relative. Can I then be given credit for common sanity? Can I make any effective excuse except Bunyan's excuse, which is no excuse at all? If I plead that I am only doing what More and Bunyan, Dickens and Wells did I do not exonerate myself: I convict them.

All I can plead is that as events as they actually occur mean no more than a passing crowd to a policeman on point duty, they must be arranged in some comprehensible order as stories. Without this there can be no history, no morality, no social conscience. Thus the historian, the story teller, the playwright and his actors, the poet, the mathematician, and the philosopher, are functionaries without whom civilization would not be possible. I conclude that I was born a story teller because one was needed. I am therefore not a disease but a social necessity.

DIVINE PROVIDENCE

Providence, which I call The Life Force; when not defeated by the imperfection of its mortal instruments, always takes care that the necessary functionaries are born specialized for their job. When no specialization beyond that of common mental ability is needed, millions of "hands" (correctly so called industrially) are born. But as they are helpless without skilled craftsmen and mechanics, without directors and deciders, without legislators and thinkers, these also are provided in the required numbers. Chaucer and Shakespear, Dante and Michael Angelo, Goethe and Ibsen, Newton and Einstein, Adam Smith and Karl Marx arrive only once at intervals of hundreds of years, whilst carpenters and tailors, stockbrokers and parsons, industrialists and traders are all forthcoming in thousands as fast as they are needed.

I present myself there as an instrument of the Life Force, writing by what is called inspiration; but as the Life Force proceeds experimentally by Trial-and-Error, and never achieves a 100 per cent success, I may be one of its complete failures, and certainly fall very short not only of perfection but of the Force's former highest achievements. For instance I am much less mentally gifted than, say, Leibniz, and can only have been needed because, as he was so gifted as to be unintelligible to the mob, it remained for some simpler soul like myself to translate his nomads and his universal substance, as he called the Life Force, into fables which, however farfetched, can at least interest, amuse, and perhaps enlighten those capable of such entertainment, but baffled by Leibniz's algebraic symbols and his philosophic jargon.

Here I must warn you that you can make no greater mistake in your social thinking than to assume, as too many do, that persons with the rarest mental gifts or specific talents are in any other respect superior beings. The Life Force, when it gives some needed extraordinary quality to some individual, does not bother about his or her morals. It may even, when some feat is required which a human being can perform only after drinking a pint of brandy, make him a dipsomaniac, like Edmund Kean, Robson, and Dickens on his last American tour. Or, needing a woman capable of bearing first rate children, it may endow her with enchanting sexual attraction yet leave her destitute of the qualities that make married life with her bearable. Apparently its aim is always the attainment of power over circumstances and matter through science, and is to this extent benevolent;

but outside this bias it is quite unscrupulous, and lets its agents be equally so. Geniuses are often spendthrifts, drunkards, libertines, liars, dishonest in money matters, backsliders of all sorts, whilst many simple credulous souls are models of integrity and piety, high in the calendar of saints.

MENTAL CAPACITY DIFFERS AND DIVIDES

When reading what follows it must not be forgotten that though we differ widely in practical ability and mental scope, the same basic income, or ration, or minimum wage, or national dividend, or whatever the newspapers call it for the moment, will suffice for mayor and scavenger, for admiral and cabin boy, for judge and executioner, for field marshal and drummer boy, for sexton and archbishop, bank manager and bank porter, sister of charity and prison wardress, and who not. What is more, they are all equally indispensable. An industrial magnate once wrote asking me did I realize that his army of laborers would be destitute and helpless without him. I replied that if he did not realize that without them he would be a nobody he was no gentleman. This closed the correspondence.

Equality of income is an obvious corollary. Yes; but how much income? A national dividend of, say, thirteen shillings a week per family, which was the share agricultural laborers got in the nineteenth century, kept them alive for thirty years or so, but left no surplus for education and culture: in short, for civilization. Now without cultured homes civilization is impossible. Without culture possible in every home democratic civilization is impossible, because equality of opportunity is impossible. The present combination of class culture and general savagery produces civil war, called class war, until strikes, lock-outs, and police batons are succeeded by shot and shell. Then the final destruction of civilization is threatened.

Consequently the basic income to be aimed at must be sufficient to establish culture in every home, and wages must be levelled up, not down, to this quota by increased production. When the quota is achieved, arithmetical inequality will no longer matter; for the eugenic test is general inter-

65

marriageability; and though the difference between £5 a week and £50 makes the recipients practically exogamous, millionaires could not marry at all if they scorned brides from homes with £5000 a year. There is no harm in a few people having some spare money, called capital, to experiment with; for the basic income will keep them in the normal grooves.

So much for the economics of the situation produced by differences in mental capacity! Having dealt with it in former writings, I mention it here only for new readers saturated with the common notion that income ought to vary with mental capacity, personal talent, and business ability. Such equations are wildly impossible, and having nothing to do with the insane misdistribution of national income produced by nineteenth century plutocracy. And so I pass on to political ethics.

Most of us so far are ungovernable by abstract thought. Our inborn sense of right and wrong, of grace and sin, must be embodied for us in a supernatural ruler of the universe: omnipotent, omniscient, all wise, all benevolent. In ancient Greece this was called making the word flesh, because the Greeks did not then discriminate between thought and the words that expressed it. The Bible translators have Englished it too literally as the word made flesh.

But as the minds of the masses could not get beyond their trades and their localities, their God could not be omnipresent; and a host of minor gods sprang up. The Greeks added to Zeus and Chronos vocational deities: Vulcan the blacksmith, Athene (Minerva) the thinker, Diana the huntress, Aphrodite (Venus) the sexmistress. They reappear in Christianity as Peter the fisherman, Luke the painter, Joseph the carpenter, Saint Cecilia the musician, and the rest.

But this also was too wide a classification for the very simple souls, who carried the localization of their gods to the extent of claiming exclusive property for their own city in each saint, and waging civil war in the name of the black image of the Blessed Virgin in their parish church against the worshippers of her white image in the next village.

FARFETCHED FABLES
SATANIC SOLUTION OF THE PROBLEM OF EVIL

A difficulty was raised by the fact that evil was in the world as well as good, and often triumphed over the good. Consequently there must be a devil as well as a divinity: Poochlihoochli as well as Hoochlipoochli, Ahriman as well as Ormudz, Lucifer Beelzebub and Apollyon as well as the Holy Trinity, the Scarlet Woman as well as Our Lady: in short as many demons as saints.

At first, however, this setting up against God of a rival deity with a contrary ideology was resented as a Manichean heresy, because plague pestilence and famine, battle murder and sudden death, were not regarded with horror as the work of Shelley's Almighty Fiend, but with awe as evidence of the terrible greatness of God, the fear of him being placed to his credit as the beginning of wisdom. The invention of Satan is a heroic advance on Jahvism. It is an attempt to solve the Problem of Evil, and at least faces the fact that evil *is* evil.

Thus the world, as we imagine it, is crowded with anthropomorphic supernatural beings of whose existence there is no scientific proof. None the less, without such belief the human race cannot be civilized and governed, though the ten per cent or so of persons mentally capable of civilizing and governing are mostly too clever to be imposed on by fairy tales, and in any case have to deal with hard facts as well as fancies and fictions.

MENDACITY COMPULSORY IN KINGCRAFT AND PRIESTCRAFT

This lands them in the quaintest moral dilemmas. It drives them to falsehoods, hypocrisies, and forgeries most distressing to their intellectual consciences. When the people demand miracles, worship relics, and will not obey any authority that does not supply them, the priest must create and nourish their faith by liquefying the blood of Saint Januarius, and saying Mass over a jawbone labelled as that of Saint Anthony of Padua. When the people believe that the earth is flat, immovable, and the centre of the universe, and Copernicus and Leonardo convince both Galileo the scientist and the Vatican that the earth is a planet of the sun, the Pope and the cardinals have to make Galileo recant and pretend that he believes what the people believe, because, if the Church admits that it has ever been mistaken, its whole authority will collapse, and civilization perish in anarchy. If Joshua could not make the sun stand still, there is a blunder in the Bible. When the Protestants blew the gaff to discredit the Vatican, and the secret could no longer be kept by forbidding Catholics to read the Bible, the people were not logical enough to draw subversive inferences. They swallowed the contradiction cheerfully.

Meanwhile the people had to be threatened with a posthumous eternity in a brimstone hell if they behaved in an uncivilized way. As burning brimstone could not hurt a spirit, they had to be assured that their bodies would be resurrected on a great Day of Judgment. But the official translators of the Bible in England were presently staggered by a passage in the Book of Job, in which that prophet declared that as worms would destroy his body, in the flesh he should not see God. Such a heresy, if published, would knock the keystone out of the arch of British civilization. There was nothing for it but to alter the word of God, making Job say that though worms would destroy his body yet in his flesh he should see God. The facts made this forgery necessary; but it was a forgery all the same.

A later difficulty was more easily got over. The apostles were Communists so Red that St Peter actually struck a man and his wife dead for keeping back money from the common stock. The translators could not pretend that St Peter was a disciple of the unborn Adam Smith rather than of Jesus; so they let the narrative stand, but taught that Ananias and Sapphira were executed for telling a lie and not for any economic misdemeanor. This view was impressed on me in my childhood. I now regard it as a much graver lie than that of Ananias.

"The lie" said Ferdinand Lassalle "is a European Power." He might, however, have added that it is none the worse when it does a necessary job; for I myself have been a faker of miracles. Let me tell one of my old stories over again.

FARFETCHED FABLES
G.B.S. MIRACLE FAKER

When I was a vestryman I had to check the accounts of the Public Health Committee. It was a simple process: I examined one in every ten or so of the receipted accounts and passed it whilst my fellow members did the same; and so enough of the accounts got checked to make their falsification too risky.

As it happened, one which I examined was for sulphur candles to disinfect houses in which cases of fever had occurred. I knew that experiments had proved that the fumes of burning sulphur had no such effect. Pathogenic bacilli like them and multiply on them.

I put the case to the Medical Officer of Health, and asked why the money of the ratepayers should be spent on a useless fumigant. He replied that the sulphur was not useless: it was necessary. But, I urged, the houses are not being disinfected at all. "Oh yes they are" he said. "How?" I persisted. "Soap and water and sunshine" he explained. "Then why sulphur?" "Because the strippers and cleaners will not venture into an infected house unless we make a horrible stink in it with burning sulphur."

I passed the account. It was precisely equivalent to liquefying the blood of Saint Januarius.

Some twenty years later I wrote a play called Saint Joan in which I made an archbishop explain that a miracle is an event that creates faith, even if it is faked for that end. Had I not been a vulgar vestryman as well as a famous playwright I should not have thought of that. All playwrights should know that had I not suspended my artistic activity to write political treatises and work on political committees long enough to have written twenty plays, the Shavian idiosyncrasy which fascinates some of them (or used to) and disgusts the Art For Art's Sake faction, would have missed half its value, such as it is.

PARENTAL DILEMMAS

The first and most intimate of the moral dilemmas that arise from differences in mental ability are not between classes and Churches, but in the daily work of bringing up children. The difference between Einstein and an average ploughman is less troublesome than the difference between children at five, at ten, and at fifteen. At five the Church catechism is only a paradigm: I learnt it at that age and still remember its phrases; but it had no effect on my conduct. I got no farther with it critically than to wonder why it obliged me, when asked what my name was, to reply that it was N or M, which was not true.

What did affect my conduct was my nurse's threat that if I was naughty or dirty the cock would come down the chimney. I confidently recommended this formula to all parents, nurses, and kindergarten teachers, as it effects its purpose and then dies a natural death, fading from the mind as the child grows out of it without leaving any psychic complexes.

But the same cannot be said for more complicated schemes of infant civilization. If they begin with Law's Serious Call, as many pious parents think they should, they may be worse than no scheme at all. I knew a man whose youth was made miserable by a dread of hell sedulously inculcated from his infancy. His reaction against it carried him into Socialism, whereupon he founded a Labor Church in which all the meetings began by calling on the speakers to pray: a demand which so took aback my Fabian colleagues that one of them began with "Heavenly Father: unaccustomed as I have been many years to address you, I *etc. etc.*" The Labor Church did not last; but the reaction did; and the last I heard of its founder was that he was helping the movement against Victorian prudery in a very practical way as a Nudist photographer, the basis of that prudery being the fact that the clothing, or rather upholstering, of Victorian women was much more aphrodisiac than their unadorned bodies.

As to the Socialist orator who parodied "Unaccustomed as I am to public speaking," he died in the bosom of the Roman Catholic Church.

I tell these anecdotes because they give an impression, better than any abstract argument could, of the way in which highly intelligent children of pious families, or of irreligious ones capable of nothing more intellectual than sport and sex, reacted against their bringing-up. One day, at a rehearsal of one of my plays, an actress who was a Roman Catholic consulted me in some distress because her adolescent son had become an atheist. I advised her not to worry; for as family religions have to be cast off as thoughtless habits before they can be replaced by genuine religious convictions, she might safely leave her son's case to God.

Edmund Gosse was the son of a Plymouth Brother, and was baptized by total immersion, of which he wrote a highly entertaining description in his book called Father and Son. The immersion had washed all the father's pious credulity out of the son. George Eliot, also piously brought up, began her reaction by translating Emil Strauss's Life of Jesus, which divested the worshipped Redeemer of supernatural attributes, and even questioned the sanity of his pretension to them.

THE ALL OR NOTHING COMPLEX

In those days we were all what I called Soot or Whitewash merchants, pilloried as All or Nothings in Ibsen's Brand. When one link in our mental chain snapped we did not pick up the sound links and join them, we threw the chain away as if all its links had snapped. If the story of Noah's Ark was a fable, if Joshua could not have delayed the sunset in the Valley of Ajalon, if the big fish could not have swallowed Jonah nor he survive in its belly, then nothing in the Bible was true. If Jehovah was a barbarous tribal idol, irreconcilable with the God of Micah, then there was no God at all, and the heavens were empty. On the other hand if Galileo, the man of science, knew better than Joshua, and Linneus and Darwin better than Moses, then everything that scientists said was true. Thus the credulity that believed in the Garden of Eden with its talking serpent, and in the speeches of Balaam's ass, was not cured. It was simply transferred to Herbert Spencer and John Stuart Mill. The transfer was often for the worse, as when baptism by water and the spirit, consecrating the baptized as a soldier and a servant of the Highest, was replaced by the poisonous rite of vaccination on evidence that could not have imposed on any competent statistician, and was picked up by Jenner from a dairy farmer and his milkmaids.

CATHOLICISM IMPRACTICABLE

The lesson of this is that a totally Catholic Church or Communist State is an impossible simplification of social organization. It is contrary to natural history. No Church can reconcile and associate in common worship a Jehovah's Witness with William Blake, who called Jehovah Old Nobodaddy. Napoleon, who pointed to the starry sky and asked "Who made all that?" did not kneel beside those who replied that it made itself, or retorted "We dont know: and neither do you." I, as a Creative Evolutionist, postulate a creative Life Force or Evolutionary Appetite seeking power over circumstances and mental development by the method of Trial and Error, making mistake after mistake, but still winning its finally irresistible way. Where in the world is there a Church that will receive me on such terms, or into which I could honestly consent to be received? There are Shaw Societies; but they are not Catholic Churches in pretence, much less in reality. And this is exactly as it should be, because, as human mental capacity varies from grade to grade, those who cannot find a creed which fits their grade have no established creed at all, and are ungovernable unless they are naturally amiable Vicars of Bray supporting any government that is for the moment established. There are hosts of such creedless voters, acting strongly as a conservative force, and usefully stabilizing government as such. But they make reforms very difficult sometimes.

THE TARES AND THE WHEAT

I therefore appreciate the wisdom of Jesus's warning to his missionaries that if they tore up the weeds they would tear up the wheat as well, meaning that if they tried to substitute his gospel for that of Moses instead of pouring the new wine into the old bottles (forgive the Biblical change of metaphor) nothing would be left of either Jesus or Moses. As I put it, the conversion of savagery to Christianity is the conversion of Christianity to savagery.

This is as true as ever. Not only are the immediate black converts of our missionaries inferior in character both to the unconverted and the born converted, but all the established religions in the world are deeply corrupted by the necessity

72

for adapting their original inspired philosophic creeds to the narrow intelligences of illiterate peasants and of children. Eight thousand years ago religion was carried to the utmost reach of the human mind by the Indian Jainists, who renounced idolatry and blood sacrifice long before Micah, and repudiated every pretence to know the will of God, forbidding even the mention of his name in the magnificent temples they built for their faith.

But go into a Jainist temple today: what do you find? Idols everywhere. Not even anthropomorphic idols but horse idols, cat odols, elephant idols and what not? The statues of the Jainist sages and saints, far from being contemplated as great seers, are worshipped as gods.

THE THIRTYNINE ARTICLES

For such examples it is not necessary to travel to Bombay. The articles of the Church of England begin with the fundamental truth that God has neither body, parts, nor passions, yet presently enjoin the acceptance as divine revelation of a document alleging that God exhibited his hind quarters to one of the prophets, and when he had resolved to destroy the human race as one of his mistakes, was induced to make an exception in the case of Noah and his family by a bribe of roast meat. Later articles instruct us to love our fellow-creatures, yet to obey an injunction to hold accursed all who do good works otherwise than in the name of Christ, such works being sinful. In one article it is at first assumed that the swallowing of a consecrated wafer is only the heathen rite of eating the god (transubstantiation) and as such abominable, and then that it is holy as a memorial of the last recorded supper of Jesus. No man can be ordained a minister of the Church of England unless he swears without any mental reservation that he believes these contradictions. I once held lightly that candidates of irresistible vocation might swear this blamelessly because they were under duress. But one day I was present at the induction of a rector. When the bishop asked the postulant to tell a flat lie which both of them knew to be a lie, and he told it without a blush, the impression made on me was so shocking that I have felt ever since that the Church of England must revise

73

its articles at all hazards if it is to be credited with the intellectual honesty necessary to its influence and authority. Shake that authority, and churchgoing will be nothing more than parading in our best clothes every Sunday.

A HUNDRED RELIGIONS AND ONLY ONE SAUCE

As it is, Christianity has split into sects, persuasions, and Nonconformities in all directions. The Statesman's Year-Book has given up trying to list them. They range from Pillars of Fire, Jehovah's Witnesses, Plymouth Brothers, and Glasites, to Presbyterians, Methodists, Congregationalists, Baptists, Friends (Quakers), and Unitarians. Within the Established Church itself there are Ritualists, Anglo-Catholics who call their services Masses and never mention the Reformation, Laodicean Broad Churchmen, and Low Church Protestants. The Friends abhor ritual and dictated prayers, and repudiate cathedral services and Masses as playacting, whilst the Anglo-Catholics cannot think religiously without them. Presbyterians and Congregationalists differ from the clergy of the Established Church on the political issue of episcopal or lay Church government. The Unitarians reject the Trinity and deny deity to Jesus. Calvinists deny universal atonement, preached by our missionaries, who are practically all Independents.

Common to these irreconcilable faiths is the pretension that each is the true Catholic Church, and should hand over all whom it cannot convert to the State (the Secular Arm) to be exterminated for the crime of heresy by the cruellest possible methods, even to burning alive. This does not mean that all rulers who order such extermination are horribly cruel. "Bloody Mary" believed that heretics must be liquidated; but she was not responsible for the political circumstance that the secular criminal law was atrociously cruel, and that no other agency could effect the liquidation. Calvin agreed that Servetus must be killed; but he objected humanely to his being burned. Charles II, humane (indeed, as some think, too humane in his kindness to his dozen dogs and half dozen mistresses), could not question the necessity for punishing the Regicides with death; but he

74

loathed the butchering of them in the hideous manner ordained centuries earlier for the punishment of William Wallace, and stopped it as soon as he dared. It was still unrepealed during my own lifetime; and has only just (1948) been repealed in Scotland.

So far I have not been imprisoned, as poorer men have been in my time, for blasphemy or apostasy. I am not technically an apostate, as I have never been confirmed; and my godparents are dead. But having torn some of the Thirtynine Articles to rags, I should have been pilloried and had my ears cropped had I lived in the days of the British Inquisition called the Star Chamber. Nowadays Nonconformity and Agnosticism are far too powerful electorally for such persecution. But the Blasphemy Laws are still available and in use against obscure sceptics, whilst I suffer nothing worse than incessant attempts to convert me. All the religions and their sects, Christian or Moslem, Buddhist or Shinto, Jain or Jew, call me to repentance, and ask me for subscriptions. I am not so bigoted as to dismiss their experiences as the inventions of liars and the fancies of noodles. They are evidence like any other human evidence; and they force me to the conclusion that every grade of human intelligence can be civilized by providing it with a frame of reference peculiar to its mental capacity, and called a religion.

THE MARXIST CHURCH

The Marxist Church, called Cominform, is like all the other Churches. Having ceased to believe in the beneficently interfering and overruling God of Adam Smith and Voltaire, no less than in the vicarage of the Pope and his infallibility in council with the College of Cardinals, Cominform makes Karl Marx its Deity and the Kremlin his Vatican. It worships his apostles at its conventicles and in its chapels, with Das Kapital as its Bible and gospel, just as Cobdenist Plutocracy used to make a Bible of Adam Smith's Wealth of Nations with its gospel of The Economic Harmonies and its policy of Free Trade.

I am myself much idolized. I receive almost daily letters from devout Shavians who believe that my income is unlimited, my knowledge and wisdom infinite, my name a guarantee of success for any enterprise, my age that of Jesus at his death, and the entire Press at my command, especially The Times, of which I am assumed to be the proprietor.

If this is not idolatry the word has no meaning. The fact that I am ascertainably, and indeed conspicuously, only a superannuated (not supernatural) journalist and play-wright does not shake the faith of my idolaters in the least. Facts count for nothing. I am told that I should be shot in Russia if I dared to pontificate against the Government there as I often do here, and that Freedom of the Press, the glory of England, does not and cannot exist under Communist tyranny.

SHOULD I BE SHOT IN RUSSIA?

As a matter of fact the Russian newspapers are full of complaints and grievances. There is a Government Depart-ment whose function it is to receive and deal with such com-plaints. Here in England I, an old journalist and agitator, know only too well that both platform and press are gagged by such an irresponsible tyranny of partisan newspaper pro-prietors and shamelessly mendacious advertizers, and by the law against seditious and blasphemous libel, that my speeches were never reported, and my letters and articles inserted only when I could combine what I believed and wanted to say with something that the paper wanted to have said, or when I could disguise it as an attractively readable art criticism, the queer result being that my reputation was made in Conservative papers whilst the Liberal, Radical, and Socialist editors dared not mention my name except in disparagement and repudiation. I owe more of my pub-licity to The Times than to any other daily newspaper. The same is true of my Fabian colleagues. The Webbs, now in Westminster Abbey, never could get into the British daily newspapers. In Russia, when Fabians were despised there as bourgeois Deviators, the Webbs were translated by Lenin.

As a playwright I was held up as an irreligious pornog-rapher, and as such a public enemy, not to say a thorough-paced cad, for many years by an irresponsible censorship which could not be challenged in parliament or elsewhere.

No such misfortune has happened to me in Russia.

What damns our foreign policy here is our ignorance of history of home affairs. In the imagination of our amateur politicians England is a Utopia in which everything and everybody is "free," and all other countries "police States." I, being Irish, know better.

To return to the inveteracy of idolatry. Ten years ago disciples of a rival celebrity were sending me portraits of an Austrian Messiah named Hitler, described by Mr Winston Churchill as a bloodthirsty guttersnipe, yet more fanatically deified in Germany than Horatio Bottomley in England.

One of the puzzles of history is whether Jesus, denounced by the ladies and gentlemen of his time as a Sabbath breaker, a gluttonous man, and a winebibber, and finally executed for rioting in the temple, really believed in his claim to be Messiah, or was forced to assume that character because he could not make converts on any other terms, just as Mahomet found that he could not govern the Arabs without inventing a very sensual paradise and a very disgusting hell to keep them in order. Whether he invented his conversations with the Archangel Gabriel, or, like Joan of Arc, really heard voices when he listened for the voice of God, we shall never know. I have just had a letter from a man who, having made repeated attempts to give up smoking and failed, until one day, walking through Hyde Park, he heard a Gospel preacher cry "Listen for the voice of God and it will come to you." This stuck in his mind. He listened, not piously but experimentally; and sure enough a voice said to him "Quit smoking: quit smoking." This time he quitted without the smallest difficulty.

COMPATIBILITIES

Differences of creed must be tolerated, analyzed, discussed, and as far as possible reconciled. My postulate of a provident and purposeful Life Force that proceeds by trial-and-error, and makes mistakes with the best intentions, is not in effect irreconcilable with belief in a supernatural benignant Providence at war with a malignant Satan. We cannot "make our souls" in the same assembly; but in the same building we can. Therefore if our cathedrals and churches are to be open to all faiths, as they in fact are, for contemplation and soul making, their different rituals must be performed at different hours, as they are at the Albert Hall in London, the Usher Hall in Edinburgh, the Free Trade hall in Manchester, the Montford Hall in Leicester, and wherever two or three gathered together may hear Messiah or the great Masses of Bach and Beethoven on Sunday or Monday, and watch a boxing show on Tuesday or Wednesday. The rituals differ, but not enough to provoke their votaries to burn one another at the stake or refuse to dine together on occasion. The sporting peer who becomes famous as the owner of a Derby winner meets the winner of a Nobel Prize without the least embarrassment; and I have never suffered the smallest discourtesy except once in a Manchester club, and then only because my criticisms of Shakespear stopped this side of idolatry.

It may seem that between a Roman Catholic who believes devoutly in Confession and a modern freethinking scientist there can be neither sympathy nor co-operation. Yet there is no essential difference between Confession and modern Psychotherapy. The post-Freudian psychoanalyst relieves his patient of the torments of guilt and shame by extracting a confession of their hidden cause. What else does the priest do in the confessional, though the result is called cure by one and absolution by the other? What I, a Freethinker, call the Life Force, my pious neighbors call Divine Providence: in some respects a better name for it. Bread and wine are changed into living tissue by swallowing and digestion. If this is not transubstantiation what *is* transubstantiation? I have described the surprise of a Fabian lecturer on being asked to open a political meeting with prayer. When I was invited to address the most important Secular Society in England I found that I had to supply the sermon in a ritual of hymns and lessons in all respects like a religious Sunday service except that the lessons were from Browning and the hymns were aspirations to "join the choir invisible." Later on, when I attended a church service in memory of my wife's sister, and was disposed to be moved by it, the les-

78

son was the chapter from the Bible which describes how the Israelites in captivity were instructed by a deified Jonathan Wild to steal the jewelry of the Egyptians before their flight into the desert. The Leicester Atheists were in fact more pious than the Shropshire Anglicans.

BOHEMIAN ANARCHISM

The anarchy which the priests feared when they gagged Galileo actually came to pass much more widely than the epidemics which the Medical Officer of Health dreaded when he gagged me about the sulphur candles. In my early days as a Socialist lecturer I was once opposed by a speaker who had been an apostle of Robert Owen's New Moral World, the first version of British Socialism. His ground was that too many of his fellow apostles took the new moral world as an emancipation from all the obligations of the old moral world, and were dishonest and licentious. Prominent in my own generation of Marxists was one who, I believe, would have gone as a martyr to the scaffold or the stake rather than admit that God existed, or that Marx and Darwin were fallible. But when money or women were concerned, he was such a conscienceless rascal that he was finally blackballed by all the Socialist societies.

Do not misunderstand me. I am not stigmatizing all Owenites, Marxists, and Darwinists as immoral; but it must be borne in mind that all revolutionary and reform movements are recruited from those who are not good enough for the existing system as well as those who are too good for it. All such movements attract sinners as well as saints by giving them a prominence as platform orators and pamphleteers out of all proportion to their numbers and deserts. They justify their delinquencies as assertions of principle, and thus give Socialism a reputation for anarchism, irreligion, and sexual promiscuity which is association of ideas, not logic. No eminence in a specific department implies even ordinary ability in any other, nor does any specific personal depravity imply general depravity. I may fairly claim to be an adept in literature; but in dozens of other departments I am a duffer. I have often quoted a certain ex-Colonel who said to me "I know for certain that the Rector is the father

79

of his housemaid's illegitimate child; and after that you may tell me that the Bible is true: I shall not believe you." It does not follow that the Colonel was not a military genius, nor the Rector an eloquent preacher and efficient clergyman.

Nevertheless we cannot legislate for every individual separately, nor provide a special policeman to keep him (or her) in order. All civilized persons except certified lunatics and incorrigible criminals must for elementary purposes be held equally capable and responsible. Those who cannot read any book more abstruse than Esop's Fables, nor get beyond the multiplication table (if so far) in mathematics, can understand the Ten Commandments well enough to be legislated for in the mass.

SHAM DEMOCRACY

In the face of these hard facts most of the current interpretations of the word Democracy are dangerous nonsense. The fundamental notion that the voice of the people is the voice of God is a sample. What people? Were Solon and Sully, Voltaire and Adam Smith, Plato and Aristotle, Hobbes and Tom Paine and Marx, the people? Were Lord George Gordon, Titus Oates, and Horatio Bottomley the people? Were General Roberts and Henry Irving, nominated by Gallup poll as ideal rulers, the people? Am I the people? Was Ruskin? Were Moses, Jesus, Peter and Paul, Mahomet, Brigham Young? If their voices were all voices of God, God must be a very accomplished ventriloquist.

Democracy means government in the interest of everybody. It most emphatically does not mean government BY everybody. All recorded attempts at that have not only failed but rapidly developed into despotisms and tyrannies. The trade union secretary elected by everybody in his Union, the pirate captain whose crew can make him walk the plank at any moment, are the most absolute despots on earth. Cromwell tried government by a parliament of elected saints and had to turn it into the street as Bismarck turned the Frankfort Parliament in 1862. He tried an oligarchy of majors general, but finally had to make himself Lord Protector and govern despotically as much as it was possible to govern Englishmen at all, which, as he bitterly complained, was not very much. Much or little, votes for everybody, politically called Adult Suffrage, always produces anarchy, which, being unbearable, produces by reaction overwhelming majorities in favor of Regressions called Restorations, or Napoleonic Emperors and South American dictator-presidents. Democratic government of the people by the people, professed ideologically nowadays by all Governments and Oppositions, has never for a moment existed.

Real democracy leaves wide open the question as to which method best secures it: monarchies, oligarchies, parliaments nominated or elected with or without proportional representation, restricted franchise, intervals between general elections, or other "checks and balances" devised to prevent glaring abuses of virtually irresponsible power. None of them has ever made Voltaire's *Monsieur Tout le Monde* master of the situation. Adult suffrage did not prevent two so-called world wars and a royal abdication on which the people were no more consulted than I was. Political adventurers and "tin Jesuses" rose like rockets to dictatorships and fell to earth like sticks, or were succeeded, as Napoleon was, by Bourbonic bosses. The Russian Bolsheviks, having invented the Soviet System, and brought their country to the verge of ruin and a little over by All or Nothing Catastrophism, were forced by the facts to make room in Bolshevism for more private enterprise than there is in England. The moment it did so, the basic difference between British and Russian economic policy vanished or crisscrossed. Lenin and Stalin had to cry *Laisser-faire* to all the enterprises not yet ripe for nationalization. The Labor Party in England nationalized as many industries as it could manage, and regulated private employers, controlled prices, rationed food and clothing, imposed purchase taxes on luxuries, and increased the bureaucracy both in numbers and power whilst jealously restricting official salaries more grudgingly with a view to equality of income than the Kremlin. Stalin's Russo-Fabian slogan, Socialism in a Single Country, is countered by Churchill's manifestos of Plutocratic Capitalism Everywhere and Down with Communism, which is more than Trotsky claimed for international Marxism.

With all this staring them in the face, and no intention whatever of going back to turnpike roads, toll bridges, private detectives and prizefighters for police, sixpenny linkmen for municipal electric lighting, cadis under palm trees for judges, condottieri and privateers for national defence, profiteers for Exchequer Chancellors: in short, the substitution of private enterprise for the omnipresent Communism without which our civilization could not endure for a week, our politicians and partisans keep shouting their abhorrence of Communism as if their Parties were cannibal tribes fighting and eating one another instead of civilized men driven by sheer pressure of facts into sane co-operation.

THE POLITICAL TIME LAG

The worst features of our sham-democratic misgovernment are caused, not by incurable mental incapacity, but by an ignorance that is essentially mathematical. None of our politicians seems to know that political action, like all earthly action, must take place in a world of four dimensions, not three. The fourth dimension is that of Time. To ignore it is to be pre-Einstein, which is as out-of-date as to be pre-Marx. Fortunately it can be taught, just as the theories of rent and value can be taught; and those who learn it see that our British parliamentary system is far too slow for twentieth century social organization. The Soviet system in Russia outstrips it because, being faster, it is more immediately responsive to the continual need for reforms and adaptations to changing circumstances. It includes all the conventional democratic checks and safeguards against despotism now so illusory, and gives them as much effectiveness as their airy nature is capable of. Incidentally it gives Stalin the best right of any living statesman to the vacant Nobel peace prize, and our diplomatists the worst. This will shock our ignoramuses as a stupendous heresy and a mad paradox. Let us see.

When the horrors of unregulated selfish private enterprise forced both Conservatives and Cobdenists to devise and pass the Factory Acts, it took the British Parliament a time lag of 50 years to make them effective. Home Rule for Ireland took thirty years to get through Parliament, and was decided after all by a sanguinary civil war.

In the simplest home affairs the time lag extends to centuries. For instance, the practice of earth burial, with its cemeteries crowding the living out by the dead, its poisonous slow putrefactions, its risk of burial alive, and its cost, should be forbidden and replaced by cremation. It was discussed 80 years ago when I was a boy. Yet not even the cremation of an Archbishop (Temple: one of our best) has overcome our dread of doing anything that everyone else is not yet doing, nor the bigoted opposition of the Churches which preach the Resurrection of The Body without considering that a body can be resurrected from dust and ashes as feasibly as from a heap of maggots. Our crematory gardens of rest are still countable only in dozens, and cremations only in thousands, even in big cities. In lesser towns the figure is zero.

ADULT SUFFRAGE IS MOBOCRACY

Adult Suffrage is supposed to be a substitute for civil war. The idea is that if two bodies of citizens differ on any public point they should not fight it out, but count heads and leave the decision to the majority. The snag in this is that as the majority is always against any change, and it takes at least thirty years to convert it, whilst only ten per cent or thereabouts of the population has sufficient mental capacity to foresee its necessity or desirability, a time lag is created during which the majority is always out-of-date. It would be more sensible to leave the decision to the minority if a qualified one could be selected and empanelled. Democratic government needs a Cabinet of Thinkers (Politbureau) as well as a Cabinet of Administrators (Commissars). Adult Suffrage can never supply this, especially in England, where intellect is hated and dreaded, not wholly without reason, as it is dangerous unless disciplined and politically educated; whilst acting and oratory, professional and amateur, are popular, and are the keys to success in elections.

83

FARFETCHED FABLES
THE MARXIST CLASS WAR
The conflict of economic interest between proprietors and proletarians was described by H. G. Wells as past and obsolete when it had in fact just flamed up in Spain from a bandying of strikes and lock-outs into raging sanguinary civil war, as it had already done in Russia, with the difference that in Russia the proletarians won, whereas in Spain they were utterly defeated through lack of competent ministers and commanders.

The struggle is confused by a cross conflict between feudal and plutocratic ideologies. The feudal proprietariat is all for well policed private property and *Laisser-faire*, the proletariat all for State industry with abolition of feudal privilege and replacement of private or "real" property by property on social conditions; so that a proprietor shall hold his land, his shares, his spare money (called capital) on the same terms as his umbrella: namely that he shall not use it to break his neighbor's head nor evict him from his country and homestead to make room for sheep or deer.

Both parties insist on the supreme necessity for increased production; but as the Plutocrats do all they can to sabotage State industry, and the Proletarians to sabotage private enterprise, the effect is to hinder production to the utmost and demonstrate the vanity of two-party government.
WHAT IS TO BE DONE?
I am asked every week what is my immediate practical remedy for all this. Also what is my solution of the riddle of the universe? When I reply that I dont know, and have no panacea, I am told that I am not constructive, implying that practical people are constructive and do know. If they are and do, why are we in our present perilous muddle?

I can only suggest certain definite and practicable experiments in social organization, on a provisional hypothesis or frame of reference (a necessary tool of thought) that will serve also as a credible religion. For nomenclatory purpose I may be called a Fabian Communist and Creative Evolutionist if I must have a label of some sort. At present I am stuck all over with labels like a tourist's trunk. I cannot call myself the Way and the Life, having only a ques-

84

tionable hypothesis or two to offer; but that is the heroic label that all Worldbetterers aspire to, and some have even dared to claim.

Some 30 years or so ago I wrote a play called As Far As Thought Can Reach. Perhaps I should have called it as far as my thought could reach; but I left this to be taken for granted.

POLITICAL MATHEMATICS

What we need desperately is an anthropometric slide-rule by which we can classify and select our rulers, most of whom are at present either rich nonentities, venal career-ists, or round pegs in square holes. Now it is no use my sing-ing at the top of my voice that democracy is impossible with-out scientific anthropometry. I might as well be the Town Crier offering a reward for an imaginary lost dog. How are we to begin?

Sixty years ago Sidney Webb created a Progressive Party on the new County Councils by sending to all the candidates at the first election a catechism setting forth a program of Socialist reforms, and demanding whether they were in favor of them or not. As Nature abhors a vacuum the program flew into empty heads and won the election for them. This, as far as I know, was the first non-party test ever applied to membership of a public authority in England since benefit of clergy was legal, and the professions were closed to all but members of the Church of England. This at least provided some evidence as to whether the candidate could read, write, and even translate a little dog Latin. It was better than no test at all.

But it is now quite insufficient in view of the enormous increase of public functions involved by modern Socialism. We already have in our professional and university exam-inations virtual panels of persons tested and registered as qualified to exercise ruling functions as Astronomers Royal, Archbishops, Lord Chief Justices, and public schoolmasters. Even police constables are instructed. Yet for the ministers who are supported to direct and control them we have no guarantee that they can read or write, or could manage a baked potato stall successfully.

85

FARFETCHED FABLES

Now people who cannot manage baked potato stalls nor peddle bootlaces successfully cannot manage public departments manned with school-tested permanent executives. Consequently these executives constitute a bureaucracy, not a democracy. Elections do not touch them: the people have no choice. When they have passed the competitive examinations by which they are tested, they are there for life, practically irremovable. And so government goes on.

Unfortunately the tests tend to exclude born rulers. Knowledge of languages, dead and foreign, puts a Mezzofanti, useless as a legislator or administrator, above a Solon who knows no language but his own. It puts facility in doing set sums in algebra by rule of thumb above inborn mathematical comprehension by statesmen who cannot add up their washing bills accurately. Examinations by elderly men of youths are at least thirty years out of date: in economics, for instance, the candidate who has been taught that the latest views are those of Bastiat and Cobden, ignoring those of Cairnes and Mill, is successful, especially if he ranks those of Karl Marx as blasphemous, and history as ending with Macaulay. The questions that will be asked and the problems set at the examinations, with the answers and solutions that will be accepted by the elderly examiners, soon become known, enabling professional crammers to coach any sixth form schoolboy to pass in them to the exclusion of up-to-date candidates who are ploughed because they know better than their examiners, yet are as unconscious of their mental superiority as a baby is of the chemistry by which it performs the complicated chemical operation of digesting its food.

Evidently the present curriculum and method should be radically changed. When I say this, the reply is "Granted; but how?" Unfortunately I dont know; and neither does anyone else; but as somebody must make a beginning here are a few of the best suggestions I can think of.

RENT AND VALUE THE ASS'S BRIDGES

First, there is the economic Ass's Bridge: the theory of rent, and with it inextricably the theory of exchange value. Unless a postulant for first class honors in politics can write an essay shewing that he (or she) has completely mastered

86

these impartial physical and mathematical theories, the top panel must be closed against him. This would plough Adam Smith, Ricardo, Ruskin, and Marx; but they could read up the subject and return to the charge. Stanley Jevons would pass it, though after he had knocked out Ricardo and the rest with his correct mathematical theory he taught that a State parcel post is an impossibility. For when he returned to England after serving in the Gold Escort in Australia, and became a university professor, he taught anything and everything the old examiners expected him to teach, and so might have failed in a character test.

STATISTICS VITAL

The panel for health authorities should require a stringent test in statistics. At present the most unbearable tyranny is that of the State doctor who has been taught to prescribe digitalis and immobilization, plus a diet of alcoholic stimulants, for heart disease, and to amputate limbs and extirpate tonsils as carpenters and plumbers deal with faulty chair legs and leaking pipes. He may, like Jenner, be so ignorant of the rudiments of statistics as to believe that the coincidence of a decrease in the number of deaths from a specific disease following the introduction of an alleged prophylactic proves that the prophylactic is infallible and that compulsion to use it will abolish the disease. Statisticians, checking the figures by the comparisons they call controls, may prove up to the hilt that the prophylactic not only fails to cure but kills. When vaccination was made compulsory as a preventive of smallpox the controls were cholera, typhus, and endemic fever: all three rampant when I was born. They were wiped out by sanitation; whilst under compulsory vaccination, enforced by ruthless persecution, smallpox persisted and culminated in two appalling epidemics (1871 and 1881) which gave vaccination its deathblow, though its ghost still walks because doctors are ignorant of statistics, and, I must add, because it is lucrative, as it calls in the doctor when the patient is not ill. In the army some thirty inoculations are practically compulsory; and vaccination is made a condition of admission to the United States and other similarly deluded countries. The personal outrage involved

87

is so intolerable that it will not be in the least surprising if vaccination officers are resisted, not with facts and figures but with fists, if not pistols.

The remedy, however, is not to compel medical students to qualify as statisticians, but to establish a Ministry of Statistics with formidable powers of dealing with lying advertisements of panaceas, prophylactics, elixirs, immunizers, vaccines, antitoxins, vitamins, and professedly hygienic foods and drugs and drinks of all sorts. Such a public department should be manned not by chemists analyzing the advertized wares and determining their therapeutical value, but by mathematicians criticizing their statistical pretensions. As there is an enormous trade in such wares at present the opposition to such a Ministry will be lavishly financed; but the need for it is too urgent to allow any consideration to stand in its way; for the popular demand for miracles and deities has been transferred to "marvels of science" and doctors, by dupes who think they are emancipating themselves from what in their abysmal ignorance they call medieval barbarism when they are in fact exalting every laboratory vivisector and quack immunizer above Jesus and St James. Mrs Eddy, a much sounder hygienist than Jenner, Pasteur, Lister, and their disciples, had to call her doctrine Christian Science instead of calling the popular faith in pseudo-scientific quackery Anti-Christian Nonsense.

THE ESTHETIC TEST

The next test I propose may prove more surprising. For the top panel I would have postulants taken into a gallery of unlabelled reproductions of the famous pictures of the world, and asked how many of the painters they can name at sight, and whether they have anything to say about them, or are in any way interested in them. They should then be taken into a music room furnished with a piano, and asked to sing or whistle or hum or play as many of the leading themes of the symphonies, concertos, string quartets, and opera tunes of Mozart and Beethoven, and the Leitmotifs of Wagner, as they can remember. Their performances may be execrable; but that will not matter: the object is not to test their executive skill but to ascertain their knowledge of the best music and their interest in and enjoyment of it, if any.

I would have them taken then into a library stocked with the masterpieces of literature. They should be asked which of them they had ever read, and whether they read anything but newspapers and detective stories. If the answer be Yes, they can be invited to indicate the books they know.

I am quite aware of the possibility of misleading results. Dr Inge, an unquestionably top notcher, when he was Dean of St Paul's and had to deal with the music there, expressed a doubt whether the Almighty really enjoys "this perpetual serenading." William Morris, equally *honoris causa*, could not tolerate a piano in his house. When one was played in his hearing by his neighbors, he would throw up his window and roar curses at them.

But if Dr Inge had been brought up on Beethoven instead of on Jackson's Te Deum, he might have preferred Wagner to Plotinus; and Morris was deeply affected by medieval music, and quite right in loathing the modern steel grand piano of his day as a noisy nuisance. Still, some of the postulants will be tone deaf or color blind. Their comments may be none the less valuable as evidence of their mental capacity.

SUBCONSCIOUS CAPACITIES

More baffling at present are the cases in which the judges will be faced with apparently vacant minds, and met, not with an epigram of which no mediocrity would be capable, but with a blank "I dont know what you are talking about." This will not prove that the postulant is a nitwit: it will raise the question whether the question is beyond his mental powers or so far within them that he is unconscious of them. Ask anyone how water tastes, and you will get the reply of Pinero's Baron Croodle "Water is a doglike and revolting beverage" or simply "Water has no taste," or, intelligently, "Water has no taste for me, because it is always in my mouth." Ask an idle child what it is doing, and it will not claim that it is breathing and circulating its blood: it will say it is doing nothing. When we co-ordinate our two eyes to look at anything we do not notice that the images of everything else within our range of vision are doubled. When we listen to an orchestra or an organ we are deaf to the accompanying thunder of beats, partials, and harmonics. Attention is a condition of consciousness. Without it we may miss many "self-evident truths." How then are we to distinguish between the unconscious genius and the idiot?

Again, I do not know; but we can at least call in the professional psychotherapists whose business it is to dig up the buried factors of the mind and bring them to light and consciousness. The technique of this therapy has developed since the days when, being asked what the word Ass suggested to me, I replied Dogberry and Balaam. It suggested, not facts and experiences, but fictions. Put the word Calculus to a surgeon and he will name the disease called stone, from which Newton suffered. Put it to a mathematician and he will cite the method of measurement Newton and Leibniz elaborated.

EXAMINATIONS AND SCHOOLMASTERS

I avoid calling the tests examinations because the word suggests the schoolmaster, the enemy of mankind at present, though when by the rarest chance he happens to be a born teacher, he is a priceless social treasure. I have met only one who accepted my challenge to say to his pupils "If I bore you you may go out and play." Set an average schoolmaster or schoolmarm to test for the panels, and the result will be a set of examination papers with such questions and problems as "Define the square root of minus one in Peano terms; and if an empty aeroplane travelling at supersonic speed takes a thousand light years to reach the nearest star, how long will it take a London motor bus keeping schedule time to travel from Millbank to Westminster Bridge with a full complement of passengers? Give the name, date, and locality of the birth of Beethoven's great grandmother's cousin's stepsister; and write a tonal fugue on the following theme. Give the family names of Domenichino and Titian; and write an essay not exceeding 32 words on their respective styles and influence on Renaissance art. Give the dates of six of Shakespear's plays, with the acreage occupied by (*a*) the Globe Theatre, (*b*) the Shoreditch Curtain the-

atre, and (*c*) the Blackfriars theatre. Estimate the age of
Ann Hathaway at her marriage with Shakespear. Enumer-
ate the discrepancies between the narratives of Homer,
Plutarch, Holinshed, and Shakespear. Was Bacon the author of Shakespear's plays (5000 words)?"

THE WRONG SORT OF MEMORY

And so on. The schoolmaster does not teach. He canes
or impositions or "keeps in" the pupils who cannot answer
pointless questions devised to catch them out. Such questions test memory, but secure victory in examinations for the
indiscriminate encyclopedic memory, which is the most dis-
abling of all memories. Universities are infested with ped-
ants who have all recorded history at their tongues' ends,
but can make no use of it except to disqualify examinees
with the priceless gift of forgetting all events that do not
matter. Were I to keep always in mind every experience
of my 93 years living and reading I should go mad. I am
often amazed when, having to refer to old papers filed away
and forgotten, I am reminded of transactions which I could
have sworn had never occurred, and meetings with notable
persons I have no recollection of having ever seen. But this
does not disconcert me. Kipling's "Lest we forget" is often
less urgent than "Lest we remember."

Certainly, those who forget everything are impossible
politically; and I have often wished I had the memory of
Macaulay or Sidney Webb, or the patience of my player
collaborators who have to memorize speeches I have myself
written but of which at rehearsal I cannot quote two words
correctly; but on the whole the people who remember
everything they ought to forget are, if given any authority,
more dangerous than those who forget some things they
had better remember. Dr Inge, commenting on the Irish
question, pointed out how difficult is the common government of a nation which never remembers and one which
never forgets.

Anyhow, we must keep schoolmasters away from the
panel tests. My own school experience has biased me on
this point. When the time came to teach me mathematics I
was taught simply nothing: I was set to explain Euclid's

diagrams and theorems without a word as to their use or history or nature. I found it so easy to pick this up in class that at the end of the half year I was expected to come out well in the examinations. I entirely disgraced myself because the questions did not pose the propositions but gave only their numbers, of which I could recollect only the first five and the one about the square of the hypothenuse.

The next step was algebra, again without a word of definition or explanation. I was simply expected to do the sums in Colenso's schoolbook.

Now an uninstructed child does not dissociate numbers or their symbols from the material objects it knows quite well how to count. To me a and b, when they meant numbers, were senseless unless they meant butter and eggs and a pound of cheese. I had enough mathematical faculty to infer that if $a = b$ and $b = c$, a must equal c. But I had wit enough to infer that if a quart of brandy equals three Bibles, and three Bibles the Apostles' Creed, the Creed is worth a quart of brandy, manifestly a *reductio ad absurdum*.

My schoolmaster was only the common enemy of me and my schoolfellows. In his presence I was forbidden to move, or to speak except in answer to his questions. Only by stealth could I relieve the torture of immobility by stealthily exchanging punches (called "the coward's blow") with the boy next me. Had my so-called teacher been my father, and I a child under six, I could have asked him questions, and had the matter explained to me. As it was, I did exactly what the Vatican felt everybody would do if Galileo picked a hole in the Bible. I concluded that mathematics are blazing nonsense, and thereafter made a fool of myself even in my twenties when I made the acquaintance of the editor of Biometrika, Karl Pearson, who maintained that no theory could be valid until it was proved mathematically. I threw in his teeth my conviction that his specialty was an absurdity. Instead of enlightening me he laughed (he had an engaging smile and was a most attractive man) and left me encouraged in my ignorance by my observation that though he was scrupulous and sceptical when counting and correlating, he was as credulous and careless as any ordinary mortal in selecting the facts to be counted. Not until Graham Wallas, a born teacher, enlightened me, did I understand mathematics and realize their enormous importance.

SOME RESULTS

Is it to be wondered at that with such school methods masquerading as education, millions of scholars pass to their graves unhonored and unsung whilst men and women totally illiterate or at most selftaught to read and write in their late teens, rise to eminence whilst "university engineers" are drugs in the labor market compared to those who go straight from their elementary schools to the factory, speaking slum English and signing with a mark. Experienced employers tell us they prefer uneducated workmen. Senior Wranglers and Double-Firsts and Ireland Scholars see no more than costermongers in the fact that a saving of 1 per cent per minute of time in writing English means 525,000 per cent per year, and that ten times that much could be saved by adding 15 letters to the alphabet. It took a world war to establish summer time after it had been contemptuously rejected by our pundits as a negligible fad. The fact that by adding two digits to our arithmetic tables we could make 16 figures do the work of twenty (a colossal saving of time for the world's bookkeeping) appeals no more to winners of the mathematical tripos than the infinitesimal calculus to a newly born infant. Political controversy is now (1949) raging on the nationalization of our industries; yet not one word is said nor a figure given as to its basic advantage in the fact that coal can be had in Sunderland for the trouble of picking it up from the sands at low tide, whilst in Whitehaven it has to be hewn out under the sea, miles from the pit head, or that land in the City of London fetches fabulous prices per square foot and twenty miles off will hardly support a goose on the common, thus making it impossible without nationalization to substitute cost-of-production prices, averaged over the whole country, for prices loaded with enormous rents for the proprietors of London land and Seaham mines, not equivalently surtaxed. Doctors and dental surgeons who excuse their high fees on the ground that they are working until half past four in the afternoon earning rent for their land-lords, and only the rest of the day for themselves and their families, are so incapable of putting two and two together politically that they vote like sheep for the landlords, and denounce land municipalization as robbery. Had the late famous President Franklin Roosevelt, a thoroughly schooled gentleman-amateur Socialist, been taught the law of rent, his first attempts at The New Deal would not have failed so often. I could cite dozens of examples of how what our Cabinet ministers call Democracy, and what I call Mobocracy, places in authority would-be rulers who assure us that they can govern England, plus the Commonwealth, plus Western Europe, and finally the world, when as a matter of fact they could not manage a village shop success-fully.

CAPITAL ACCUMULATION

Capital is spare money saved by postponement of con-sumption. To effect this in a private property system some people must be made so rich that when they are satiated with every purchasable luxury they have still a surplus which they can invest without privation. In the nineteenth century this arrangement was accepted as final and inevitable by able and benevolent public men like Thomas de Quincey, Ma-caulay, Austin, Cobden, and Bright, until Karl Marx dealt it a mortal blow by shewing from official records that its delusive prosperity masked an abyss of plague, pestilence and famine, battle, murder, compulsory prostitution, and premature death. Ferdinand Lassalle in Germany had al-ready demonstrated the injustice of its "iron law of wages."

ENGLAND'S SHAMEFACED LEADERSHIP

England was by no means silent on the subject. Marx's invective, though it rivalled Jeremiah's, was pale beside the fierce diatribes of Ruskin, who puzzled his readers by describing himself as an old Tory and the Reddest of Red Communists. Carlyle called our boasted commercial pros-perity shooting Niagara, and dismissed Cobdenist Free Trade as Godforsaken nonsense. The pious Conservative Lord Shaftesbury and the Radical atheist demagogue Brad-laugh were at one in their agitation for Acts in restraint of the prevalent ruthless exploitation of labor. Robert Owen had called for a New Moral world as loudly as any of our present post war Chadbands. It was he who made current the word Socialism as the alternative to Capitalist plutocracy. When the Russian Bolsheviks went ruinously wrong by ignoring "the inevitability of gradualness" and attempting a catastrophic transfer of industry and agriculture from private to public ownership, it was the Englishman Sidney Webb and his Fabians who corrected them and devised the new economic policy Lenin had to announce, and Stalin to put in practice. Thus Englishmen can claim to have been pioneers in the revolutionary development of political organization since Cobdenism conquered us.

Unfortunately, whenever English parties effect an advance, they are so ashamed of it that they immediately throw away all credit for it by protesting that they are respectable citizens who would never dream of changing anything, and shouting their abhorrence of all the wicked foreigners who are in effect taking their advice. And then they are surprised when their disciples, especially in Russia, regard them as enemies, and the Marxist Left wins more and more votes from them.

THE THREATENING FUTURE: HOMILIES NO USE

While the time lag lasts the future remains threatening. The problem of optimum wealth distribution, which Plutocracy, with its inherent class warfare, has hopelessly failed to solve, will not yield to the well-intentioned Utopian amateurs who infest our parliaments and parties, imagining that it can be solved by giving all of us according to our needs and balancing the account by taking from each of us according to our productive capacity. They might as well decree that we shall do unto others as we would have them do to us, or achieve the greatest good for the greatest number, or soothe our souls with exhortations to love oneanother. Homilies cut no ice in administrative councils: the literary talent and pulpit eloquence that has always been calling for a better world has never succeeded, though it has stolen credit for many changes forced on it by circumstances and natural selection. The satirical humor of Aristophanes, the wisecracks of Confucius, the precepts of the Buddha, the parables of Jesus, the theses of Luther, the *jeux d'esprit* of Erasmus and Montaigne, the Utopias of More and Fourier and Wells, the allegories of Voltaire, Rousseau, and Bunyan, the polemics of Leibniz and Spinoza, the poems of Goethe, Shelley, and Byron, the manifesto of Marx and Engels, Mozart's Magic Flute and Beethoven's Ode to Joy, with the music dramas of Wagner, to say nothing of living seers of visions and dreamers of dreams: none of these esthetic feats have made Reformations or Revolutions; and most of them, as far as they have been thrown into the hands of the common people as the Protestant Reformation threw the Bible, have been followed by massacres, witch hunts, civil and international wars of religion, and all forms of persecution, from petty boycotts to legalized burnings at the stake and breakings on the wheel, highly popular as public entertainments. The nineteenth century, which believed itself to be the climax of civilization, of Liberty, Equality, and Fraternity, was convicted by Karl Marx of being the worst and wickedest on record; and the twentieth, not yet half through, has been ravaged by two so-called world wars culminating in the atrocity of the atomic bomb.

As long as atomic bomb manufacture remains a trade secret known to only one State, it will be the mainstay of Peace because all the States (including the one) will be afraid of it. When the secret is out atomic warfare will be barred as poison gas was in 1938–45; and war will be possible as before. How that may happen is the subject of the first two farfetched fables that follow.

Ayot Saint Lawrence,
   1948–9

FIRST FABLE

A PUBLIC *park on a fine summer afternoon. Chairs for hire scattered about the sward.*

A young woman of respectable appearance arrives and seats herself. A park attendant approaches her; takes two-pence from her; says "Kew," short for "Thankyou"; and gives her a ticket.

A well-dressed young man enters and takes the nearest chair. The attendant takes two-pence as before, and passes on.

YOUNG MAN. Excuse me. Would you rather I sat farther away?

YOUNG WOMAN. As you please. I dont care where you sit.

YOUNG MAN. I hope you dont think me intrusive?

YOUNG WOMAN. I am not thinking about you at all. But you may talk to me if you want to. I dont mind.

YOUNG MAN. Well, I certainly do want to talk to you. In fact that is why I took this chair.

YOUNG WOMAN. I thought so. Well, talk away. What have you to say to me?

YOUNG MAN. Ive never seen you before. But at first sight I find you irresistibly attractive.

YOUNG WOMAN. Lots of men do. What of it?

YOUNG MAN. Some women find me attractive. Are you married?

YOUNG WOMAN. No. Are you?

YOUNG MAN. No. Are you engaged?

YOUNG WOMAN. No. What is it to you whether I am engaged or not?

YOUNG MAN. Need you ask? Ive got into this conversation with a view to our possible marriage.

YOUNG WOMAN. Nothing doing. I'll not marry.

YOUNG MAN. It is odd that so many attractive women are unmarried. Dull ugly frumps never seem to have any difficulty in finding mates. Why wont you marry? I am available.

YOUNG WOMAN. My father was shot in the Great War

that now seems such a little one. My eldest brother was killed in Normandy when we were liberating France there. His wife and children were blown to bits by a bomb that wrecked the whole street they lived in. Do you think I'll bear children for that?

YOUNG MAN. They died for England. They made war to end war. Dont you admire bravery? Dont you love your country?

YOUNG WOMAN. What use is bravery now when any coward can launch an atomic bomb? Until men are wise and women civilized they had better not be born. At all events I shall not bring them into this wicked world to kill and be killed.

An excited middle-aged man comes along waving a newspaper and cheering.

M. A. M. Hurrah! Have you heard the news?

YOUNG MAN. No. Whats happened?

M. A. M. No more war. The United Nations have abolished it.

YOUNG MAN [*disparagingly*] Hmm! May I have a look at your paper?

M. A. M. Here it is in black and white. You may keep it. I'll buy another. Hurrah! hurrah!! hurrah!!!

He hands over the paper and rushes away, cheering.

YOUNG WOMAN. What does it say?

YOUNG MAN [*reading the headlines*] "THE WORLD AT PEACE AT LAST. WASHINGTON AGREES. MOSCOW AGREES. CHINA AGREES. THE WESTERN UNION AGREES. THE FEDERALISTS AGREE. THE COMMUNISTS AGREE. THE FASCISTS AGREE. ATOMIC BOMB MANUFACTURE MADE A CAPITAL CRIME. UNIVERSAL SECURITY GUARANTEED."

YOUNG WOMAN. Have the armies been disbanded? Have the military academies been closed? Has conscription been abolished?

YOUNG MAN. It doesnt say. Oh yes: here is a stop press paragraph. "ARMIES WILL IN FUTURE BE CALLED WORLD POLICE. NO MORE CONSCRIPTION." Hm!

YOUNG WOMAN. You dont seem pleased.

YOUNG MAN. I dont swallow all that rot about no more

war. Men will always fight even if they have nothing to
fight with but their fists. And the women will egg them on.

YOUNG WOMAN. What does the leading article say?

YOUNG MAN [*turning to the leader page and quoting*]
"Truce of God begins a new chapter in the history of the
globe. The atomic bomb has reduced war to absurdity; for
it threatens not only both victors and vanquished but the
whole neutral world. We do not as yet know for certain that
the bomb that disintegrated Hiroshima is not still at work
disintegrating. The weather has been curiously unusual
ever since. But no nation will ever venture on atomic warfare again."

YOUNG WOMAN. Do you believe that?

YOUNG MAN. Yes; but it wont stop war. In 1914 the
Germans tried poison gas; and so did we. But the airmen
who dropped it on the cities could not stay in the air for
long; and when they had to come down they found the
streets full of the gas, because poison gas is heavier than
air and takes many days to disperse. So in the last war gas was
not used; and atomic bombs wont be used in the next one.

YOUNG WOMAN. Oh! So you think there will be a next
one.

YOUNG MAN. Of course there will, but not with atomic
bombs. There is no satisfaction in seeing the world lit up
by a blinding flash, and being burnt to dust before you have
time to think about it, with every stick and stone for miles
around falling and crumbling, all the drains and telephones
and electrics torn up and flung into the air, and people who
are too far off to be burnt die of radiation. Besides, bombs kill
women. Killing men does not matter: the women can re-
place them; but kill the women and you kill the human
race.

YOUNG WOMAN. That wont stop war. Somebody will discover a poison gas lighter than air! It may kill the inhabitants of a city; but it will leave the city standinig and in
working order.

YOUNG MAN [*thoughtfully, letting the newspaper drop
on his knees*] That is an idea.

YOUNG WOMAN. What idea?

YOUNG MAN. Yours. There is a lot of money in it. The Government gave £100,000 to the man who found out how to land our army in Normandy in 1945.

YOUNG WOMAN. Governments will pay millions for any new devilment, though they wont pay twopence for a washing machine. When a Jewish chemist found out how to make high explosive cheaply we made him a present of Jerusalem, which didnt belong to us.

YOUNG MAN [*hopefully*] Yes, by George! So we did.

YOUNG WOMAN. Well, what of it?

YOUNG MAN. I'm a chemist.

YOUNG WOMAN. Does that mean that you are in the atomic bomb business?

YOUNG MAN. No; but I'm on the staff in a chlorine gas factory. The atomic bomb people may be barking up the wrong tree.

YOUNG WOMAN [*rising wrathfully*] So that is what you are! One of these scientific devils who are destroying us! Well, you shall not sit next me again. Go where you belong: to hell. Good day to you.

She goes away.

YOUNG MAN [*still thoughtful*] Lighter than air, eh? [*Slower*] Ligh—ter—than—air?

The scene fades out.

SECOND FABLE

A ROOM *in the War Office in London. The Commander-in-Chief at work reading letters. A secretary opening them. The telephone rings. The secretary answers it.*

SEC. Yes? . . . [*To the C.-in-C.*] Lord Oldhand from the Foreign Office.

C.-IN-C. Shew him up; and get out.

SEC. He is shewing himself up. He must have heard—

Lord O. bursts in. The secretary hurries out.

OLDHAND. Ulsterbridge: have you heard the news?

C.-IN-C. Of course Ive heard the news. Here in the War Office we have to get the news in six minutes. At the Foreign Office six years is soon enough for you. Sit down.

OLDHAND [*seating himself*] Is this a time for your Irish jokes? What the devil are we to do? How much do you know?

C.-IN-C. Only that there is not one of God's creatures left alive in the Isle of Wight. I shall have to send every soldier in England to cremate the dead or throw them into the sea. The Home Office will have to find 88,454 civilians to dust the houses with vacuum cleaners and keep the banks and the telephone services and the wireless and water supplies and the lighting and the markets and all the rest of it going.

OLDHAND. Precisely. And all this is your fault.

C.-IN-C. Oldhand: you lie, categorically. How my fault?

OLDHAND. Do you forget that when that fellow who found out how to make volatile poison gas offered us his discovery it was you who turned him down?

C.-IN-C. That cockney blighter? He wanted a hundred thousand pounds for it. And the scientific authorities assured me that every penny spent on anything but atomic research would be wasted.

OLDHAND. Well, he sold it to the South African negro Hitler, Ketchewayo the Second, for a hundred and fifty thousand. Ketch could afford it: his backyard is chock full of diamonds. The fellow made a Declaration of Independ-

ence for Zululand with himself as emperor. Capetown,
Natal, and Rhodesia went to war with him and involved us
in it. That made it your job, didnt it?

C.-IN-C. Not a bit of it. Ketch is far too cunning to go
to war with us. He did not go to war with anybody. He
dropped his bombs on the Isle of Wight just to shew Capetown and the rest that the world was at his mercy. He
selected the Isle of Wight because it's a safe distance from
his own people, just as we selected Hiroshima in 1945. He
thinks islands are out-of-the-way little places that dont matter to us. But he maintains that his relations with the Commonwealth are friendly; and as you have not declared war
on him we are still technically at peace. That makes it your
job, not mine, though as usual when there is anything to be
done except what was done last time, I shall have to do it.

OLDHAND. You have a very important diplomatic point
there, I admit; but it must stand over. Meanwhile let us
put our heads together and get to work. The first practical
step is to hang this traitor who has sold his accursed invention to the enemy.

C.-IN-C. What! Dont you know that he went to live in
the Isle of Wight as the safest civilized place in the world,
and is now lying dead there, killed by his own poison gas?

OLDHAND. Serve the scoundrel right! there is the hand
of God in this. But your mistake in turning the fellow down
was none the less a mistake because he is dead and you are
alive—so far. You may be dead tomorrow.

C.-IN-C. So may you.

OLDHAND. Yes; and it will be your doing.

C.-IN-C. How was I to know that the gas was any good?
I get dozens of such inventions every week, all guaranteed
to make an end of war and establish heaven on earth. I'm a
soldier, not a chemist. I have to go by what the scientific
authorities tell me. Youre a diplomatist, not a laboratory
bloke. Do you know what an isotype is? Do you know what
a meson is? I dont: neither do you. What could you have
done except what I did? kick the fellow out.

OLDHAND. Listen to me. I am, as you say, a diplomatist;
and I think youll admit that I know my job after my fifteen

years in the Foreign Office. You know your job too as a soldier: I dont question it. That gives us one great principle in common.

c.-in-c. And what is that, may I ask?

OLDHAND. It is to regard all our allies as Powers that may at any moment become our enemies. The public thinks it is the other way about; but we know better. We must be prepared for war before everything.

c.-in-c. We never are, thanks to the damned taxpayers who wont vote us the money. But of course I agree in principle. What then?

OLDHAND. I'll tell you what then. What sort of fellow was this volatile gas man? You interviewed him. What did you make of him?

c.-in-c. Oh, a middleclass cad through and through. Out for money and nothing else. Big money.

OLDHAND. Just so. Well, what security have we that after selling his invention to Ketchewayo in Africa he did not sell it over again in Europe? All he had to do was to hand over half a sheet of notepaper with a prescription on it and pocket another hundred and fifty thousand. Every State in Europe and America except ourselves may have it up its sleeve for all we know. The gas may come in at that window while we are talking.

c.-in-c. That is true: it may. Let us hope it wont.

OLDHAND. Hope wont help us if it does. Our first duty is at all cost to get hold of that receipt, and make the gas ourselves. When the other States know that we have plenty of it none of them will dare to start using it. Meanwhile—

c.-in-c. Meanwhile I have to provide gas masks for everybody in the country, and make wearing of them compulsory. I have to bury the dead; and I cant spare enough soldiers to do it. Youll have to buy a million vultures from Bombay to pick the bones of the dead before they stink us out. We must make every house in the country gas-proof, and rigidly enforce the closing of all windows. We must— [*he is interrupted by a siren alarm, followed by an artillery salvo*]. What the devil is that?

OLDHAND. Nothing. We have ordered a salute of five

guns to celebrate the hundred and first birthday of the President of the Board of Trade.

The siren screams again.

C.-IN-C. [*singing drowsily*]
"Oh we dont want to lose you;
But we think you ought to go."

He collapses, apparently into a deep sleep.

SHOUTS WITHOUT. Shut the windows! Shut the windows! Gas! Gas! *Another salvo.*

Oldhand rises and rushes toward the open window to shut it. He staggers, and can only clutch at the sill to steady himself.

OLDHAND [*with a vacant grin which develops into a smile of radiant happiness, sings*] "It's a long way to Tipperary—"

He falls dead.

THIRD FABLE

A PLEASANT *spot in the Isle of Wight. A building of steel and glass is inscribed* ANTHROPOMETRIC LABORATORY. *On the terrace before it a bench and chairs. Seated in conference are a middle-aged gentleman in a gay pullover and broadly striped nylon trousers, and two women: a comely matron in a purple academic gown, and a junior in short-skirted overall and blue slacks.*

A tourist comes along. His embroidered smock and trimmed beard proclaim the would-be artist. He stops on seeing the three, and produces a camera.

THE GIRL. Hello! What are you doing here?

THE TOURIST. Only hiking round the island. May I take a snapshot?

THE GIRL. You have no business to be here. You have no business to be on the Isle of Wight at all. Who let you land?

THE TOURIST. I came in my own boat. I landed on the beach. What harm am I doing?

THE GIRL. This is a colony of the Upper Ten. Anybodies are not allowed here.

THE TOURIST. I'm not an Anybody: I'm classed as a Mediocrity.

THE GIRL. Neither Mediocrities nor Anybodies are admitted. Go back to your boat; and clear out.

THE MATRON. Stop. You say you are classed as a Mediocrity. Did you pass with honors?

THE TOURIST. No. They were grossly unfair to me. I'm not a Mediocrity: I'm a genius.

THE MATRON. Indeed! Have you a job of any sort?

THE TOURIST. No. They offered me a job as hospital porter because I'm physically strong. How utterly beneath me! When I told them I am a genius and shewed them my drawings, they offered to make me a housepainter. I dont want to paint houses: my destiny is to paint temples in fresco.

THE GENTLEMAN [*amused*] Like Michael Angelo, eh?

THE TOURIST. Oh, I can do better work than Michael

Angelo. He is out of date. I am ultra-modern.

THE GENTLEMAN [*to the Matron*] The very man for us.

THE MATRON [*to the Tourist*] You are quite sure that you are a genius, are you?

THE TOURIST. Quite. I dont look like a bank clerk, do I?

THE MATRON. Well, we have no temples here for you to paint; but we can offer you a job that will enable you to support yourself and have enough leisure to paint what you like until the world recognizes your genius.

THE TOURIST. What sort of work will I have to do? I warn you I cant pass examinations; and I hate being regulated and disciplined. I must have perfect freedom.

THE MATRON. Anthropometric work is what we do here. Classifying men and women according to their abilities. Filling up their qualification certificates. Analyzing their secretions and reactions and so on. Quite easy laboratory work.

THE TOURIST. That will suit me down to the ground. I'm a first-rate judge of character.

THE MATRON. Splendid. Take this in to the office at the end of the passage on the right. You can have tea in the canteen when they have settled with you. [*She hands him a ticket*].

THE TOURIST [*hungrily*] Thank you.

He takes the ticket and goes into the laboratory.

THE GENTLEMAN. He will be a heaven-sent treasure.

THE GIRL. I dont agree. He seems to me to be a conceited fool who thinks himself a genius.

THE GENTLEMAN. Exactly. We shall go by his secretions and reactions: not by his own notions.

A young man in rags, unshaven, and disreputable looking, comes along.

THE GIRL. Who is this awful looking tramp? [*To him*] Hello! Who are you; and what are you doing here?

HE. I'm doing nothing here because nobody will give me anything to do. I'm devilishly hungry. Have you by any chance a crust of bread to spare?

THE MATRON. How did you get into this island? Why were you allowed to land?

HE. I was a stowaway, madam. They wanted to send me

back; but the captain of the return boat would not take me: he said I was too dirty and probably infectious and verminous. The medical officer quarantined me; but I convinced him that I am only a harmless tramp, fit for nothing better; so he let me go. And here I am.

THE MATRON. Do you do nothing to earn your bread?

THE TRAMP. I ask for it. People mostly give it to me. If not, I sing for it. Then they give me a penny or two to stop singing and go away. It's a way of life like any other. It suits me. I'm good for nothing else.

THE GENTLEMAN. How do you know you are good for nothing else?

THE TRAMP. Well, what else am I good for? You can take me into your laboratory and try if you like. There is a canteen there, isnt there?

THE GENTLEMAN. I see you are not unintelligent. You are not uneducated. You could surely work for your living.

THE TRAMP. No. Anything but that. Working is not living. If you are on that tack you wont give me anything: I know your sort. Good morning. [*He starts to go*].

THE GIRL. Stop. You are hungry. I'll get you some bread. [*She goes into the laboratory*].

THE TRAMP. Look at that, now! Ask; and it shall be given to you.

THE GENTLEMAN. Listen to me. I'll give you five guineas if youll submit to a test of your capacity in our laboratory.

THE TRAMP. It would be robbing you. I tell you I have no capacity. I'm an out-and-out Goodfornothing. And five guineas is too much to give a tramp. I must live from hand to mouth. All the joy of life goes when you have five guineas in your pocket.

THE GENTLEMAN. You need not keep it in your pocket. You can buy a decent suit of clothes with it. You need one badly. You are in rags.

THE TRAMP. Of course I'm in rags. Who would give alms to a well-dressed man? It's my business to be in rags.

THE GENTLEMAN. Very well. I'll have you arrested and put through the laboratory and classified. That is the law, compulsory for everybody. If you refuse you may be classed as irresponsible. That means that youll be enlisted in the military police or kept under tutelage in a Labor Brigade. Or you may be classed as dangerous and incorrigible, in which case youll be liquidated.

THE TRAMP. I know all that. What good will it do you? Why are you offering me five guineas when you have only to call the police and put me through the mill for nothing?

THE GENTLEMAN. You have ability enough to cross-examine me. You may have administrative ability, and be cunning enough to shirk its responsibilities. You may be one of the Artful Dodgers who know that begging is easier and happier than bossing.

THE TRAMP. Ha! ha! ha! You suspect me of being a heaven-born genius! Very well: test me til you are black in the face. Youll only be wasting your time; but that wont hurt me, because time is of no value to me: it's my profession to waste it. Youll find I can do nothing. Mind: I'm not a fool: youre quite right there; but I'm a duffer, a hopeless duffer. I can always see what the other fellows ought to do; but I cant do it. Ive tried my hand at everything: no use: Ive failed every time. Ive tastes but no talents. I'd like to be a Shakespear; but I cant write plays. I'd like to be a Michael Angelo or a Raphael; but I can neither draw nor paint. I'd love to be a Mozart or a Beethoven; but I can neither compose a symphony nor play a concerto. I envy Einstein his mathematical genius; but beyond the pence table I cant add two and two together. I know a lot, and can do nothing. When I tell the clever chaps what to do, they wont do it, and tell me I'm ignorant and crazy. And so I am: I know it only too well. Youd better give me a meal or the price of one, and let me jog on the footpath way. My name's not Prospero: it's Autolycus.

THE GENTLEMAN. If you know what other people ought to do, youll be too busy telling them, and making laws for them, to do any of it yourself. In with you into the canteen; and get your bread there.

THE TRAMP. I fly for the bread. You are the boss here: the archpriest, chooser of rulers, lord of human destiny. And your choice is a government of tramps! Ha! ha! ha! ha! ha! ha! ha! [*He goes into the laboratory roaring with laughter*].

THE GENTLEMAN. Two big catches for today. A nincompoop who thinks he's a genius; and a genius who thinks he's a nincompoop.

THE MATRON. I prefer nincompoops. I can always depend on them to do what was done last time. But I never know what a genius will be up to next, except that it will be something upsetting.

FOURTH FABLE

T*HE same place in the Isle of Wight: but the building is now inscribed* DIET COMMISSIONERS. *A Commissioner in cap and gown sits at a writing table talking into a dictaphone. He has earphones hanging from his ears.*

COMMISSIONER. What I am going to dictate is for the printer; so keep a carbon copy. It is for the new edition of my book on Human Diet. Are you ready? . . . Right. The heading is Chapter four. Living on Air. Now for the text. Ahem!

In the twentieth century the tribes of New Zealand had, under the influence of British colonists, left off eating their prisoners of war. The British themselves, influenced by a prophet whose name has come down to us in various forms as Shelley, Shakespear, and Shavius, had already, after some centuries of restricted cannibalism in which only fishes, frogs, birds, sheep, cows, pigs, rabbits, and whales were eaten, been gradually persuaded to abstain from these also, and to live on plants and fruits, and even on grass, honey, and nuts: a diet which they called vegetarian. Full stop. New paragraph. Ahem!

As this change saved the labor of breeding animals for food, and supported human health and longevity quite as well, if not better, than the eating of dead animals, it was for some time unchallenged as a step forward in civilization. But some unforeseen consequences followed. When cattle were no longer bred and slaughtered for food, milk and butter, cheese and eggs, were no longer to be had. Grass, leaves, and nettles became the staple diet. This was sufficient for rude physical health. At the Olympic Games grass eating athletes broke all the records. This was not surprising, as it had long been known that bulls and elephants, fed on grass and leaves, were the strongest, most fertile, most passionate animals known. But they were also the most ferocious, being so dangerous that nobody dared cross a field in which a bull was loose, and every elephant had to have an armed keeper to restrain it. It had also been noticed that

110

human vegetarians were restless, pugnacious, and savagely abusive in their continual controversies with the remaining meat eaters, who found it easy and pleasant to lead sedentary lives in stuffy rooms whilst the vegetarians could not live without much exercise in the fresh air. When grass eating became general men became more ferocious and dangerous than bulls. Happily they also became less capable of organized action of any kind. They could not or would not make political alliances, nor engage in industrial mass production or wage world wars. Atomic bombs and poison gases and the like were quite beyond their powers of cooperation: their ferocities and animosities, like those of the bull, did not go beyond trespassers within sight and reach. With the ending of wars their numbers increased enormously; but to the few born thinkers who still cropped up among them and ruled them as far as they were capable of being ruled, it was apparent that they were changing into supergorillas through eating grass and leaves. And though they lived longer than the meat eaters, they still suffered from certain deadly diseases and from decay of teeth, failure of eyesight, and decrepitude in old age. Their ablest biologists had to agree that the human race, having tried eating everything on earth that was eatable, had found no food that did not sooner or later poison them. This was challenged by a Russian woman, a noted vegetarian athlete. She pointed out that there was a diet that had not been tried: namely, living on air and water. The supergorillas ridiculed her, alleging that air is not food: it is nothing; and mankind cannot live on nothing in empty space. But a famous mathematician shewed just then that there is no such thing as nothing, and that space is not emptiness and in fact does not exist. There is substance, called matter, everywhere: in fact, the universe consists of nothing else; but whether we can perceive it, or eat and drink it, depends on temperature, rate of radiation, and the sensitiveness of the instruments for detecting and measuring it. As temperature rises, water changes from solid ice to liquid fluid, from liquid fluid to steam, from steam to gas; but it is none the less substantial even at temperatures that are quite immeasurable and hardly conceivable. It followed logically that living on air is as possible as living on flesh or on grass and chopped carrots, though as men cannot live under water, nor fishes out of it, each phase of substance has its appropriate form of life and diet and set of habits. Such creatures as angels are as possible as whales and minnows, elephants and microbes.

The Russian woman claimed that she had lived for months on air and water, but on condition that the air was fresh and that she took the hardest physical exercise daily. It was already known that the vigils and fasts of saints did not weaken them when their spiritual activity was intense enough to produce a state of ecstasy. Full stop: new paragraph.

This briefly is the history of the epoch-making change in social organization produced by the ending of the food problem which had through all recorded history made men the slaves of nature, and defeated all their aspirations to be free to do what they like instead of what they must. The world became a world of athletes, artists, craftsmen, physicists, and mathematicians, instead of farmers, millers, bakers, butchers, bar tenders, brewers, and distillers. Hunger and thirst, which had for centuries meant the need for bread and onions, cheese and beer, beef and mutton, became a search for knowledge of nature and power over it, and a desire for truth and righteousness. The supergorilla became the soldier and servant of Creative Evolution. Full stop. Postscript.

Stop typing and listen to instructions. What I have just dictated is for the tenth edition of my primer for infant schools in the rudimentary biology series. I have dictated only the full stops at the end of the paragraphs. I will fill in the commas and colons and semicolons on the typescript. Leave the type and the format and the illustrations to the printer: he is a better artist in books than I am. He will need paper for two hundred million copies. Goodbye.

He takes off his headphones; puts the cover on the dictaphone; sighs with relief at having done a tedious job; and goes into the building.

FIFTH FABLE

THE scene is unchanged; but the building is now labelled GENETIC INSTITUTE. *On the terrace, seated round a table loaded with old books, are four persons of uncertain age, apparently in the prime of life. Two of them are male, one female, the fourth a hermaphrodite. They wear white sleeveless tunics like heralds' tabards on which are embroidered different flower designs, the two men being distinguished by a thistle and a shamrock respectively, the woman by a rose, and the hermaphrodite by an elm with a vine round its trunk. The sleeves of the men are red, of the woman green, of the hermaphrodite the two colors in a chequered harlequin pattern. The men are close-cropped and cleanshaven: the woman's hair is dressed like that of the Milo Venus. They are in animated discussion, each with an open book on which they occasionally thump to emphasize their points.*

SHAMROCK. I cannot make head or tail of this nineteenth century stuff. They seem to have considered our business unmentionable, and tried to write books about it in which it was not mentioned. [*He shuts the book impatiently.*]

ROSE. That seems hardly possible. Our business is the very first business of any human society: the reproduction of the human race, the most mentionable subject in the world and the most important.

SHAMROCK. Well, Ive been through every scrap of nineteenth century writing that remains; and I tell you that their textbooks on physiology dont mention the reproductive organs nor hint at such a thing as sex. You would not guess from them that it existed.

HERM. To say nothing of hermaphrodites. Being myself a hermaphrodite I have looked myself up in the nineteenth century books; and I simply wasnt there.

THISTLE. Oh, they were the damnedest fools: it is impossible to understand how they kept going for a week, much less for years. They had not brains enough to make an alphabet capable of spelling their language. They counted their goods in twelves but could not count their money in more than tens because they had only ten fingers and could not invent the two missing figures. They could not change their working hours by the sun oftener than twice a year; and it took one of the worst of the killing matches they called wars to make them go even that far. Their calendar is incomprehensible: they could not fix their festivals nor make their months tally with the moon. In music their keyboards had only twelve notes in the octave instead of our sixty-four. One would think they might at least have managed nineteen to play their babyish thirds and sixths bearably in tune. They wasted millions of hours every day because they could not or would not do the simplest things; and when their five per cent of geniuses made wonderful machines for them: big machines that could rise from the ground and fly, and little ones that could think and calculate, they accepted them as gifts from some imaginary paradise they called heaven. When one of their bodily organs went wrong they did not set it right: they just cut it out, and left the patient to recover from the shock or die. When the patient was ill all over and could not be cut to pieces they dosed him with poisons: I hunted out a case of a well-known woman who was given nine different poisons for some trouble they called typhoid. The amazing thing is that she survived it. She must have had the constitution of a bear. It was in the nineteenth century that they gave up believing in idols and priests, and took to believing in medicine men and surgeons. Let us drop digging into this past that is unconceivable, and start from what we really know of the present.

He shuts his book and throws it away.

SHAMROCK [*shutting his book*] Agreed. But why did they consider sex unmentionable?

ROSE. Simply because their methods were so disgusting that they had no decent language for them. You think their methods were like ours, and their passions like ours. You could not make a greater mistake. The seminal fluids which our chemists make in the laboratory, and which it is our business to experiment with, were unknown to them: they had to use glandular excretions from the living body to perpetuate the race. To initiate births they had to practise per-

114

sonal contacts which I would rather not describe. Strangest of all, they seem to have experienced in such contacts the ecstasies which are normal with us in our pursuit of knowledge and power, and culminate in our explorations and discoveries. The religions they believed in were so wildly absurd that one would suppose they could believe anything.

SHAMROCK. Oh, come! They must have had some common sense or they couldnt have lived.

ROSE. They had gleams of it. In spite of their sensual ecstasies, they had decency enough to reserve their highest veneration for persons who abstained from them, exalting them under the special titles of saints, nuns, priests, angels, gods and the like.

HERM. Not always. There were people called Greeks who had dozens of gods whose adventures were scandalously sensual. They poisoned an old man for trying to teach their young men to reason. Serve him right, too; for some of his reasonings were sheer logomachies: in England called puns.

ROSE. True. Another set of them, called Jews or Israelites, tortured a young man to death for trying to persuade them that the divinity they worshipped was in themselves, and promising that if they killed him he would rise from the dead and establish a kingdom of righteousness not among angels in the clouds but on earth among human men and women.

HERM. That was not why they killed him: they believed anyone who promised that much. They killed him because he made a riot in their temple and drove out the money changers, whom he mistook for thieves, being too young and not enough of a financier to know how useful and necessary they were to pilgrims. His name was Hitler, poor chap!

ROSE. All the same, utterly as we are unlike these primitive savages, we are descended from them; and though we manufacture ourselves scientifically, we are not yet agreed as to the sort of mankind we ought to make, nor how many at a time, nor how long they ought to last. We all want the Just Man Made Perfect; but when our chemists ask us for an exact prescription of the necessary protoplasms, hormones, vitamins, enzymes and the rest, we never agree on the last milligram of each ingredient; and it is that milligram that determines whether the resulting product will be a poet or a mathematician.

HERM. I'm against all that. It revolts me. I tell you again and again we shall never make decent human beings out of chemical salts. We must get rid of our physical bodies altogether, except for stuffed specimens in the Natural History Museum. I dont want to be a body: I want to be a mind and nothing but a mind. In the sixteenth century men made it their first article of religion to worship a god who had neither body, parts, nor passions: sensual passions. Even in the dark ages of the nineteenth and twentieth centuries there was a man who aspired to be a vortex in thought, and a woman who declared that the mind made the body and not the body the mind. Demolish all the laboratories. Build temples in which we can pray and pray and pray for deliverance from our bodies until the change occurs naturally as all real changes do.

ROSE. My child, how much farther would that take us? We should still be unable to agree on what sort of mind we needed. Prayer, we know, is a great creative power; but to pray effectively you must know what to pray for. In the sixteenth century there was a famous mathematician who declared that our utmost knowledge was no more than a grain of sand picked up on the margin of the ocean of our ignorance. He was a silly fellow who thought that the world was only forty centuries old and that straight lines were ethically right; but the utmost that we know is still no more than his grain of sand. I would like to be a mind without a body; but that has not happened to me yet; and meanwhile, as another sixteenth sage said, the world must be peopled; and as we can no longer endure the old unmentionable methods we must make material citizens out of material substances in biochemical laboratories. I was manufactured that way myself; and so were you, my boy.

HERM. My body was, and my mind such as it is. But my desire to get rid of my body was not. Where did that come from? Can you tell me?

ROSE. No; but when we know even that, it will be only another grain of sand on the seashore. But it will be worth picking up; and so will all the other grains.

SHAMROCK. In the infinity of time, when the oceans dry up and make no more sand, we shall pick them all up. What then?

ROSE. The pursuit of knowledge and power will never end.

SIXTH AND LAST FABLE

As before, except that the building is now labelled

SIXTH FORM SCHOQL

SCHEDULED HISTORIC MONUMENT

On the terrace are five students in class, wearing uni-
forms with six sleeve stripes. Their individual numbers are
on their caps. Numbers 1, 2, 3, are youths. 4 and 5 are
maidens. Number 1 is older than number 2, number 4 than
number 5.

The teacher, a matron, in cap and gown, enters from the
building and takes her place.

TEACHER. Let me introduce myself. You have just been
promoted to the sixth form. I am your teacher. Explain to
me how and why the sixth form differs from the fifth.

YOUTH 1. We shall explain nothing to you. If you are
our teacher it is for us to question you: not for you to question us.

MAIDEN 5. Do not be prehistoric. Savages thousands of
years ago schooled their children by asking them conundrums and beating them if they could not answer them. You
are not going to start that game on us, are you?

YOUTH 3. If you do, Mother Hubbard, youll not have
a happy time with us.

TEACHER. You are quite right. It is what I expected you
to say. My question was a test. Three of you have shewn
that you understand the relation between us as teacher and
pupils in the sixth form. The rest of you, if you also agree,
will signify the same in the usual manner.

All the students raise their hands in assent.

TEACHER. Good. Now fire away. Ask your questions.

YOUTH 3. What questions shall we ask?

TEACHER. Aha! You see it is not so easy to ask questions.
Is there nothing you want to know? If not, the sixth form
is not for you: it is out of your mental range; and you can
go back to the fifth form and take your leaving certificate.

YOUTH 3. Oh I say! Give me time to think of something.

118

TEACHER. Two minutes; or back to the fifth you go.

YOUTH 2 [*prompting*] Ask her whether when a pine cone disappears into the ground it is the ground that wraps the pine cone up or the cone that buries itself into the clay.

TEACHER. Good, Number Two. I dont know; and neither does anyone else. And you, Number Three, do you really want to know?

YOUTH 3. No. I didnt know that cones bury themselves; and I dont care a dump whether they do or not.

TEACHER. Dont care a dump is vulgar. You should say dont care a dam.

YOUTH 3. Oh, I'm not literary. What does dam mean?

TEACHER. It means a negligible trifle.

YOUTH 2. Wrong, Teacher. My Dark Ages dictionary defines it as a form of profanity in use among clergymen.

TEACHER. In the sixth form, the teacher is always wrong.

YOUTH 1. You are both wrong. It means an animal's mother.

MAIDEN 5. No it doesnt. It means a wall across a river valley to pen it up as a lake.

YOUTH 3. All I meant is what the teacher says.

TEACHER. And so the teacher is always right. For announcing this, Number Three, I'll give you another minute to ask me a question that you do really care about.

YOUTH 3. Why are you so down on me? I am not the only one who hasnt a question ready for you.

TEACHER. The sixth form should be bursting with questions. I'll come to the others presently. I pick on you because your looks do not suggest more than fifth form brains.

YOUTH 1. Dont look at his face. Look at his fingers.

TEACHER. Fingers are not brains.

YOUTH 3. Yes they are. My brains are in my fingers: yours are only in your head. Have you ever invented a machine and constructed it?

TEACHER. No. Have you?

YOUTH 3. Yes.

TEACHER. How?

YOUTH 3. I dont know. I cant find words for it: I'm no talker. But I can do things. And I wont go down to the fifth.

Here I am and here I stick, whatever you say.

TEACHER. So you shall. You know your own mind, though you cannot speak it.

YOUTH 3. I have no mind. I can only do things.

MAIDEN 4. I have a question, Teacher.

TEACHER. Out with it.

MAIDEN 4. How is it that the things that come into Number Three's head never come into mine? Why can he do things that I cant do? Why can I do things that he cant do? I can write an essay: he cant write even a specification of the machines he invents. If you ask him to, he can only twiddle his fingers as if they were wheels and levers? He has to employ a Third Form patent agent to describe it for him.

TEACHER. Ah, now we are coming to the riddle of the universe. You young things always ask it, and will not take "I dont know" for an answer. Can any of you tell me the story of the Sphinx?

MAIDEN 5. I can. The Sphinx was a quadruped with a woman's head and breasts, who put conundrums to everyone who came along, and devoured them if they could not answer them.

TEACHER. Yes: that is the story. But where is the interest of it for you?

MAIDEN 5. Well, a story is a story. I like stories.

MAIDEN 4. She does, Teacher: she is always reading them. And she tells stories about herself. All lies.

YOUTH 2. Why does she tell lies? That is what I want to know.

YOUTH 3. The Sphinx story is rot. Why should the Sphinx eat everybody who couldnt answer its riddles?

YOUTH 1. Why should it kill itself if anyone did answer them? Tell me that.

TEACHER. Never ask why. Ask what, when, where, how, who, which; but never why. Only first form children, who think their parents know everything, ask why. In the sixth form you are supposed to know that why is unanswerable.

YOUTH 3. Nonsense. Why is not unanswerable. Why does water boil? Because its temperature has been raised to

100 Centigrade. What is wrong with that?

TEACHER. That is not why: it is how. Why was it boiled?

YOUTH 2. Because some fellow wanted to boil an egg and eat it. That is why.

TEACHER. Why did he want to eat it?

YOUTH 2. Because he wanted to live and not starve.

TEACHER. That is a fact, not a reason. Why did he want to live?

YOUTH 2. Like everybody else, I suppose.

TEACHER. Why does everybody want to live, however unhappily? Why does anybody want to live?

YOUTH 3. How the devil does anybody know? You dont know. I dont know.

TEACHER. Why dont we know?

YOUTH 2. Because we dont. Thats why.

TEACHER. No. Why is beyond knowledge. All the whys lead to the great interrogation mark that shines for ever across the sky like a rainbow. Why do we exist? Why does the universe exist?

YOUTH 1. If you ask me I should say the universe is a big joke.

MAIDEN 4. I do not see any fun in it. I should say it is a big mistake.

YOUTH 2. A joke must have a joker. A mistake must have a blunderer. If the world exists it must have a creator.

TEACHER. Must it? How do you know? One of the ancient gods, named Napoleon, pointed to the sky full of stars and said "Who made all that?" His soothsayers replied "Whoever it was, who made Him?"

MAIDEN 4. Or Her? Why—

TEACHER. Order, order! Let us have no more whys. They only set you chasing your own tails, like cats. Let us get to work. I call for questions beginning with how.

MAIDEN 5. How do thoughts come into our heads? I dont have a lot of thoughts like Number Four here. She is a highbrow; but I was born quite emptyheaded. Yet I get thoughts that nobody ever suggested to me. Where did they come from?

TEACHER. As to that, there are many theories. Have you

none of your own, any of you?

YOUTH 2. My grandfather lectured about the theory of the Disembodied Races. I picked it up from him when I was a kid. Of course the old man is now out-of-date: I dont take him seriously; but the theory sticks in my head because Ive never thought of anything better.

YOUTH 1. Our biology professor in the fifth swore by it. But I cannot quite stomach it.

TEACHER. Can you give me a reason for that?

YOUTH 1. Well, I was brought up to consider that we are the vanguard of civilization, the last step in creative evolution. But according to the theory we are only a survival of the sort of mankind that existed in the twentieth century, no better than black beetles compared to the supermen who evolved into the disembodied. I am not a black beetle.

YOUTH 3. Rot! If we were black beetles, the supermen would have tramped on us and killed us, or poisoned us with phosphorus.

YOUTH 1. They may be keeping us for their amusement, as we keep our pets. I told you the universe is a joke. That is my theory.

MAIDEN 5. But where do our thoughts come from? They must be flying about in the air. My father never said "I think." He always said "It strikes me." When I was a child I thought that something in the air had hit him.

YOUTH 1. What is the use of talking such utter nonsense? How could people get rid of their bodies?

TEACHER. People actually did get rid of their bodies. They got rid of their tails, of their fur, of their teeth. They acquired thumbs and enlarged their brains. They seem to have done what they liked with their bodies.

YOUTH 2. Anyhow, they had to eat and drink. They couldnt have done so without stomachs and bowels.

TEACHER. Yes they could: at least so the histories say. They found they could live on air, and that eating and drinking caused diseases of which their bodies died.

YOUTH 2. You believe that!!!

TEACHER. I believe nothing. But there is the same evidence for it as for anything else that happened millions of years before we were born. It is so written and recorded. As I can neither witness the past nor foresee the future I must take such history as there is as part of my framework of thought. Without such a framework I cannot think any more than a carpenter can cut wood without a saw.

YOUTH 2. Now you are getting beyond me, Teacher. I dont understand.

TEACHER. Do not try to understand. You must be content with such brains as you have until more understanding comes to you. Your question is where our thoughts come from and how they strike us, as Number Five's father put it. The theory is that the Disembodied Races still exist as Thought Vortexes, and are penetrating our thick skulls in their continual pursuit of knowledge and power, since they need our hands and brains as tools in that pursuit.

MAIDEN 4. Some of our thoughts are damnably mischievous. We slaughter one another and destroy the cities we build. What puts that into our heads? Not the pursuit of knowledge and power.

TEACHER. Yes; for the pursuit of knowledge and power involves the slaughter and destruction of everything that opposes it. The disembodied must inspire the soldier and the hunter as well as the pacifist and philanthropist.

YOUTH 1. But why should anybody oppose it if all thoughts come from well meaning vortexes?

TEACHER. Because even the vortexes have to do their work by trial and error. They have to learn by mistakes as well as by successes. We have to destroy the locust and the hook worm and the Colorado beetle because, if we did not, they would destroy us. We have to execute criminals who have no conscience and are incorrigible. They are old experiments of the Life Force. They were well intentioned and perhaps necessary at the time. But they are no longer either useful or necessary, and must now be exterminated. They cannot be exterminated by disembodied thought. The mongoose must be inspired to kill the cobra, the chemist to distil poisons, the physicist to make nuclear bombs, others to be big game hunters, judges, executioners, and killers of all sorts, often the most amiable of mortals outside their specific functions as destroyers of vermin. The ruthless fox-hunter loves dogs: the physicists and chemists adore their children and keep animals as pets.

YOUTH 2. Look here, Teacher. Talk sense. Do these disembodied thoughts die when their number is up, as we do? If not, there can hardly be room for them in the universe after all these millions of centuries.

MAIDEN 5. Yes: that is what I want to know. How old is the world?

TEACHER. We do not know. We lost count in the dark ages that followed the twentieth century. There are traces of many civilizations that followed; and we may yet discover traces of many more. Some of them were atavistic.

MAIDEN 5. At a what?

TEACHER. Atavistic. Not an advance on the civilization before it, but a throw-back to an earlier one. Like those children of ours who cannot get beyond the First Form, and grow up to be idiots or savages. We kill them. But we are ourselves a throw-back to the twentieth century, and may be killed as idiots and savages if we meet a later and higher civilization.

YOUTH 1. I dont believe it. We are the highest form of life and the most advanced civilization yet evolved.

YOUTH 2. Same here. Who can believe this fairy tale about disembodied thoughts? There is not a scrap of evidence for it. Nobody can believe it.

MAIDEN 4. Steady, Number Two: steady. Lots of us can believe it and do believe it. Our schoolfellows who have never got beyond the third or fourth form believe in what they call the immortality of the soul.

YOUTH 1 [*contemptuously*] Yes, because they are afraid to die.

TEACHER. That makes no difference. What is an immortal soul but a disembodied thought? I have received this morning a letter from a man who tells me he was for nineteen years a chain smoker of cigarets. He had no religious faith; but one day he chanced on a religious meeting in the park, and heard the preacher exhorting his flock to listen to

124

the voice of God. He said it would surely come to them and guide them. The smoker tried the experiment of listening just for fun; and soon his head was filled with the words "Quit smoking. Quit smoking." He quitted without the least difficulty, and has never smoked since, though he had tried before and always failed. What was that but the prompting of a disembodied thought? Millions of our third and fourth form people believe it.

YOUTH 2. Well, I am sixth form; and I dont believe it. Your correspondent is just a liar.

MAIDEN 4. What rubbish you talk, Number Two! Do fourth form people let themselves be eaten by lions in the circus, burnt at the stake, or live lives of unselfish charity rather than stop telling lies? It is much more likely that you are a fool.

YOUTH 2. May be; but that does not answer the question.

MAIDEN 5. Hear hear! The smoker may be a liar or Number Two a fool; but where did the thoughts come from? What puts them into our heads? The preachers say they are whispered by God. Anyhow they are whispered; and I want to know exactly how.

TEACHER. Like all young things you want to begin by knowing everything. I can give you only the advice of the preachers: listen until you are told.

A youth, clothed in feathers like a bird, appears suddenly.

TEACHER. Hullo! Who are you? What are you doing here?

THE FEATHERED ONE. I am an embodied thought. I am what you call the word made flesh.

YOUTH 3. Rats! How did you get here? Not by your wings: you havnt got any. You are a Cockyolly Bird.

THE FEATHERED ONE. I do not fly: I levitate. Call me Cockyolly if you like. But it would be more respectful to call me Raphael.

MAIDEN 4. Why should we respect you in that ridiculous costume?

THE TEACHER. Do you seriously wish us to believe that

you are one of the disembodied, again incarnate?

RAPHAEL. Why not? Evolution can go backwards as well as forwards. If the body can become a vortex, the vortex can also become a body.

THE TEACHER. And you are such a body?

RAPHAEL. I am curious to know what it is like to be a body. Curiosity never dies.

MAIDEN 4. How do you like it so far?

RAPHAEL. I do not like nor dislike. I experience.

YOUTH 3. That nonsense will not go down here, Cocky. It sounds smart enough; but it means nothing. Why should we respect you?

RAPHAEL. You had better. I am restraining my magnetic field. If I turned it on it would kill you.

MAIDEN 5. Dont provoke him, Number Three. I feel awful.

MAIDEN 4. You cannot experience bodied life unless you have a girl, and marry, and have children, as we do. Have you brought a girl with you?

RAPHAEL. No. I stop short of your eating and drinking and so forth, and of your reproductive methods. They revolt me.

MAIDEN 4. No passions, then?

RAPHAEL. On the contrary: intellectual passion, mathematical passion, passion for discovery and exploration: the mightiest of all the passions.

THE TEACHER. But none of our passions?

RAPHAEL. Yes. Your passion for teaching.

YOUTH 2. Then you have come to teach us?

RAPHAEL. No. I am here to learn, not to teach. I pass on. [*He vanishes*].

ALL [*screaming*] Hi! Stop! Come back! We have a lot to ask you. Dont go yet. Wait a bit, Raphael.

YOUTH 3. No use. He has invented some trick of vanishing before he is found out. He is only a Confidence Trick man.

THE TEACHER. Nonsense! He did not ask us for anything.

MAIDEN 4. He was just sampling us.

YOUTH 1. He told us nothing. We know nothing.

YOUTH 3. Rot! You want to know too much. We know how to make cyclotrons and hundred inch telescopes. We have harnessed atomic energy. He couldn't make a safety pin or a wheelbarrow to save his life.

THE TEACHER. Enough. We can never want to know too much. Attention! [*All rise*]. You will get at the schoolbook counter copies of an old poem called The Book of Job. You will read it through; and—

YOUTH 2. I read it through when I was thirteen. It was an argument between an old josser named Job and one of the old gods, who pretended he had made the universe. Job said if so he had made it very unfairly. But what use is all that to me? I dont believe the old god made the universe.

TEACHER. You will read the book over again from the point of view that the old god made no such pretence, and crushed Job by shewing that he could put ten times as many unanswerable questions to Job as Job could put to him. It will teach you that I can do the same to you. All will read the book and ask questions or write essays before next Friday.

A jubilant march is heard.

TEACHER. Lunch. March. [*Beating time*] Left-right, left-right, left-right.

They tramp out rhythmically.

SHAKES VERSUS SHAV

A PUPPET PLAY

LIII

1949

PREFACE

THIS in all actuarial probability is my last play and the climax of my eminence, such as it is. I thought my career as a playwright was finished when Waldo Lanchester of the Malvern Marionette Theatre, our chief living puppet master, sent me figures of two puppets, Shakespear and myself, with a request that I should supply one of my famous dramas for them, not to last longer than ten minutes or thereabouts. I accomplished this feat, and was gratified by Mr Lanchester's immediate approval.

I have learnt part of my craft as conductor of rehearsals (producer, they call it) from puppets. Their unvarying intensity of facial expression, impossible for living actors, keeps the imagination of the spectators continuously stimulated. When one of them is speaking or tumbling and the rest left aside, these, though in full view, are invisible, as they should be. Living actors have to learn that they too must be invisible while the protagonists are conversing, and therefore must not move a muscle nor change their expression, instead of, as beginners mostly do, playing to them and robbing them of the audience's undivided attention.

Puppets have also a fascination of their own, because there is nothing wonderful in a living actor moving and speaking, but that wooden headed dolls should do so is a marvel that never palls.

And they can survive treatment that would kill live actors. When I first saw them in my boyhood nothing delighted me more than when all the puppets went up in a balloon and presently dropped from the skies with an appalling crash on the floor.

Nowadays the development of stagecraft into filmcraft may destroy the idiosyncratic puppet charm. Televised puppets could enjoy the scenic backgrounds of the cinema. Sound recording could enable the puppet master to give all his attention to the strings he is manipulating, the dialogue being spoken by a company of first-rate speakers as in the theatre. The old puppet master spoke all the parts himself in accents which he differentiated by Punch-and-Judy squeaks and the like. I can imagine the puppets simulating living performers so perfectly that the spectators will be completely illuded. The result would be the death of puppetry; for it would lose its charm with its magic. So let reformers beware.

Nothing can extinguish my interest in Shakespear. It began when I was a small boy, and extends to Stratford-upon-Avon, where I have attended so many bardic festivals that I have come to regard it almost as a supplementary birthplace of my own.

No year passes without the arrival of a batch of books contending that Shakespear was somebody else. The argument is always the same. Such early works as Venus and Adonis, Lucrece, and Love's Labour's Lost, could not possibly have been written by an illiterate clown and poacher who could hardly write his own name. This is unquestionably true. But the inference that Shakespear did not write them does not follow. What does follow is that Shakespear was not an illiterate clown but a well read grammar-schooled son in a family of good middle-class standing, cultured enough to be habitual playgoers and private entertainers of the players.

This, on investigation, proves to be exactly what Shakespear was. His father, John Shakespear, Gent, was an alderman who demanded a coat of arms which was finally granted. His mother was of equal rank and social pretension. John finally failed commercially, having no doubt let his artistic turn get the better of his mercantile occupation, and leave him unable to afford a university education for William, had he ever wanted to make a professional scholar of him.

These circumstances interest me because they are just like my own. They were a considerable cut above those of Bunyan and Cobbett, both great masters of language, who nevertheless could not have written Venus and Adonis nor Love's Labour's Lost. One does not forget Bunyan's "The Latin I borrow." Shakespear's standing was nearer to Ruskin's, whose splendid style owes much more to his mother's insistence on his learning the Bible by heart than to his Oxford degree.

132

SHAKES VERSUS SHAV

So much for Bacon-Shakespear and all the other fables founded on that entirely fictitious figure Shaxper or Shagsper the illiterate bumpkin.

Enough too for my feeling that the real Shakespear might have been myself, and for the shallow mistaking of it for mere professional jealousy.

Ayot Saint Lawrence,
    1949

SHAKES VERSUS SHAV

SHAKES enters and salutes the audience with a flourish of his hat.

SHAKES. Now is the winter of our discontent
Made glorious summer by the Malvern sun.
I, William Shakes, was born in Stratford town,
Where every year a festival is held
To honour my renown not for an age
But for all time. Hither I raging come
An infamous impostor to chastize,
Who in an ecstasy of self-conceit
Shortens my name to Shav, and dares pretend
Here to reincarnate my very self,
And in your stately playhouse to set up
A festival, and plant a mulberry
In most presumptuous mockery of mine.
Tell me, ye citizens of Malvern,
Where I may find this caitiff. Face to face
Set but this fiend of Ireland and myself;
And leave the rest to me. [*Shav enters*]. Who art thou?
That rearst a forehead almost rivalling mine?

SHAV. Nay, who art thou, that knowest not these features
Pictured throughout the globe? Who should I be
But G. B. S.?

SHAKES. What! Stand, thou shameless fraud.
For one or both of us the hour is come.
Put up your hands.

SHAV. Come on.

They spar. Shakes knocks Shav down with a straight left and begins counting him out, stooping over him and beating the seconds with his finger.

SHAKES. Hackerty-backerty one, Hackerty-backerty two,
Hackerty-backerty   three . . . Hackerty-backerty
nine—

At the count of nine Shav springs up and knocks Shakes down with a right to the chin.

SHAV [*counting*] Hackerty-backerty one, . . . Hackerty-
backerty ten. Out.

SHAKES. Out! And by thee! Never. [*He rises*]. Younger
you are

By full three hundred years, and therefore carry
A heavier punch than mine; but what of that?
Death will soon finish you; but as for me,
Not marble nor the gilded monuments
Of princes—

SHAV.   —shall outlive your powerful rhymes.
So you have told us: I have read your sonnets.

SHAKES. Couldst write Macbeth?

SHAV. No need. He has been bettered
By Walter Scott's Rob Roy. Behold, and blush.

> *Rob Roy and Macbeth appear, Rob in Highland tar-
> tan and kilt with claymore, Macbeth in kingly costume.*

MACBETH. Thus far into the bowels of the land
Have we marched on without impediment.
Shall I still call you Campbell?

ROB [*in a strong Scotch accent*] Caumill me no Caumills.
Ma fet is on ma native heath: ma name's Macgregor.

MACBETH. I have no words. My voice is in my sword. Lay
on, Rob Roy;
And damned be he that proves the smaller boy.

> *He draws and stands on guard. Rob draws; spins round
> several times like a man throwing a hammer; and finally
> cuts off Macbeth's head at one stroke.*

ROB. Whaur's your Wullie Shaxper the noo?

> *Bagpipe and drum music, to which Rob dances off.*

MACBETH [*headless*] I will return to Stratford: the hotels
Are cheaper there. [*He picks up his head, and goes off
with it under his arm to the tune of British Grena-
diers*].

SHAKES. Call you this cateran
Better than my Macbeth, one line from whom
Is worth a thousand of your piffling plays.

SHAV. Quote one. Just one. I challenge thee. One line.

SHAKES. "The shardborne beetle with his drowsy hum."

SHAV. Hast never heard of Adam Lindsay Gordon?

SHAKES. A name that sings. What of him?

SHAV.   He eclipsed
Thy shardborne beetle. Hear his mighty lines. [*Recit-
ing*]

"The beetle booms adown the glooms
And bumps among the clumps."

SHAKES [*roaring with laughter*] Ha ha! Ho ho! My lungs
    like chanticleer
Must crow their fill. This fellow hath an ear.
How does it run? "The beetle booms—

SHAV. Adown the glooms—

SHAKES. And bumps—

SHAV. Among the clumps." Well done, Australia!
    Shav laughs.

SHAKES. Laughest thou at thyself? Pullst thou my leg?

SHAV. There is more fun in heaven and earth, sweet Wil-
    liam,
Than is dreamt of in your philosophy.

SHAKES. Where is thy Hamlet? Couldst thou write King
    Lear?

SHAV. Aye, with his daughters all complete. Couldst thou
Have written Heartbreak House? Behold my Lear.
    *A transparency is suddenly lit up, shewing Captain
    Shotover seated, as in Millais' picture called North-West
    Passage, with a young woman of virginal beauty.*

SHOTOVER [*raising his hand and intoning*] I built a house
    for my daughters and opened the doors thereof
That men might come for their choosing, and their betters
    spring from their love;
But one of them married a numskull: the other a liar
    wed;
And now she must lie beside him even as she made her
    bed.

THE VIRGIN. "Yes: this silly house, this strangely happy
    house, this agonizing house, this house without founda-
    tions. I shall call it Heartbreak House."

SHOTOVER. Enough. Enough. Let the heart break in silence.
    The picture vanishes.

SHAKES. You stole that word from me: did I not write
"The heartache and the thousand natural woes
That flesh is heir to"?

SHAV.   You were not the first
To sing of broken hearts. I was the first

SHAKES VERSUS SHAV

That taught your faithless Timons how to mend them.

SHAKES. Taught what you could not know. Sing if you can
My cloud capped towers, my gorgeous palaces,
My solemn temples. The great globe itself,
Yea, all which it inherit, shall dissolve—

SHAV.   —and like this foolish little show of ours
Leave not a wrack behind. So you have said.
I say the world will long outlast our day.
Tomorrow and tomorrow and tomorrow
We puppets shall replay our scene. Meanwhile,
Immortal William dead and turned to clay
May stop a hole to keep the wind away.
Oh that that earth which kept the world in awe
Should patch a wall t' expel the winter's flaw!

SHAKES. These words are mine, not thine.

SHAV.   Peace, jealous Bard.
We both are mortal. For a moment suffer
My glimmering light to shine.

A light appears between them.

SHAKES. Out, out, brief candle! [*He puffs it out*].
Darkness. The play ends.

THE END

138

Date Due

OCT 13 '51			
OCT 31 '51			
NOV 6 '51			
NOV 2 6 '51			
NOV 1 6 '51			
JAN 3 '52			
JAN 9 56			
MAR 1 '56			
MAR 15 '56			
JAN 5 '61			
NOV 1 '84			
Dec. 4, 65			